Always Connected for Veterans

*Deceased Vets Give Guidance
from the Other Side*

Joseph M. Higgins

*Always Connected
for Veterans
Deceased Vets Give Guidance from the Other Side*

Copyright © 2013 Joseph M. Higgins

Always Connected LLC

All Rights Reserved

No part of this book may be reproduced or transmitted in any form or by any means without written permission from the author.

ISBN-13: 978-0982571613
ISBN-10: 0982571615

Printed in U.S.A.

DISCLAIMER
The information offered in this book does not constitute a substitute for professional treatment, therapy, or other types of professional advice and intervention. If expert advice or counseling is needed, the services of a competent professional should be sought.
The information contain in this book is solely the opinion of the author and his Spiritual Guides, and should not be considered as a form of therapy, advice, direction, and/or diagnosis or treatment of any kind.

*This book is available at quantity discounts for bulk purchases.
For information, please contact www.josephmhiggins.com*

DEDICATION

This book is dedicated to all the soldiers and veterans who have served—the ones serving now, the ones who have served in the past, and those who will serve in the future—and to those who have cared for them and supported them during their time of need.

Thank you for your service and sacrifice.

ACKNOWLEDGMENTS

I would like to mention a few people who have helped me in my quest to bring peace and healing to our soldiers and veterans:

Tom Frederick, for his laughter and friendship, and for encouraging me to write this book.

DJ Harrington, for his smile, his belief that anything can be accomplished, and his thoughtfulness toward others. He walks the walk!

Nina McGurrin, for her support during the up-and-down periods and for seeing the bigger picture.

My Guides, who are always here to assist me in my thirst for knowledge and understanding.

And a special thanks to all the deceased veterans who have come together to help bring understanding, healing, and peace to all of us on the Earth plane.

CONTENTS

Introduction: Channeling Explained 1

Part I 5
  1 What we want to achieve 7
  2 Who am I and why I chose to write this book........................ 11
  3 Who they are and why they chose to write this book............. 21
  4 The process and transfer of knowledge 33
  5 Physical soldier/spiritual being 39

Part II 43
  6 Why is war necessary?.. 45
  7 Why do humans treat each other
     in such violent and indiscriminate ways 51
  8 I'm afraid that what I've done has changed me 57
  9 I can't comprehend the things I saw 63
 10 Some people think I'm a hero,
     sometimes I think I'm just crazy 71
 11 Civilians in conflict zones... 77
 12 Civilians away from conflict zones 81

Inspirational Message I 85
 13 We all don't feel this way, but some of us do 87
 14 Am I less of a soldier if I did not
     see hand-to-hand combat? 91
 15 Relationships and how they're affected................................... 97
 16 Being brave doesn't mean not having to ask for help 103
 17 Will God judge me for killing others? 109
 18 When it's my time to cross over,
     will I see the people I killed?.. 117
 19 I feel the suffering that I inflicted upon people.................... 123

Inspirational Message II 129
 20 Finding one's purpose after war 131
 21 How helping others can help you heal 137

22	How anxiety and stress can be disruptive to the learning process	143
23	POW/MIA	149
24	Dealing with injuries	159
25	Why did I go to war?	167
26	Feeling guilty, feeling nothing	173

Inspirational Message III 177

27	As a civilian, how can I talk to a combat soldier when he comes home?	179
28	How do I tell my family and others about what I have experienced?	183
29	It's hard to acclimate back into society	189
30	Suicide: Ending one's own life	195
31	Suicide: Understanding the death of a loved one	203
32	Leadership	211
33	It's not all serious	217

Part III 223

34	Healing	225
35	Concentrating on the whole self, not just the physical body	231
36	The physical tour ends, and your new spiritual tour begins	237
37	Author comments	241
38	Always connected	245

Healing Statements Guide 247

Part IV 257

Websites 259
Products 261

- *Hello…Anyone Home?*
- *The Everything Guide to Evidence of the Afterlife*

Introduction

CHANNELING EXPLAINED

The concept of channeling is best explained by my guides in my first book, *Hello ... Anyone Home?*

"As for the technological explanation of how a channel works, that is something that we can explain to a certain extent, but at times it may seem to be discombobulated.

"We have analyzed the thought waves and mechanisms that Joseph's biological structure uses on a daily basis. Further, we try to interact with these thought patterns in order to mix our thoughts in with them so that he might understand the information that is coming from our side.

"Once there was a general recognition of how Joseph's particular pattern works, we were able to intercede and stimulate certain mechanisms that alerted him about our presence. Over time and with much patience and practice, Joseph has learned to accept our invitation to communicate. He has trained himself to put his conscious focus to one side so that we may input data into his conscious mind for him to transcribe and understand.

"We see that this method of communicating is much more efficient than other methods, such as communication through dreams, as the information that we need for him to transfer is of such an amount that single, individual contacts would prohibit this process."

The channeling process at times may seem to be redundant. The guides and teachers will often repeat certain concepts in different ways in order for this information to be accepted by the largest number of readers. Many times this is very important information, which is why it is repeated with a slightly new twist. My guides and teachers have learned the best method of communicating this knowledge through me to the reader. It is up to the reader to understand the importance of these concepts and how they are presented in comparison with the information of that particular chapter.

I have tried to limit the amount of editing of the material due to its source. I wanted to share with the reader the direct information that came through my channeling sessions, so the editing process was used primary for grammar, verb tense, and to make the words flow a little more smoothly.

While writing this book, I have gained a tremendous amount of insight into the interactions of soldiers and their families. The ability to tap in and obtain this information from deceased vets in such a joyful collaboration was eye-opening. I hope it is received with the respect that it deserves.

If you're open to these concepts, use them and share them with others. If you are not able to accept the transcribed information, pass along this book to a friend, colleague, or family member, for they may have a different outlook on the concepts used to gain this knowledge and might be able to use this information to bring healing and comfort to themselves and others.

PART I

Chapter 1
WHAT WE WANT TO ACHIEVE

Those who read this book will have an opportunity to realize that their position—their existence—is part of a larger picture of life. This means that their actions and reactions have influenced the outcome of certain events. It is not for them to know why these events have occurred, but we will explain why and how they should deal with their experiences. Sometimes veterans have a difficult time understanding the position they have been put in, even though they know that the job they have to do could and does involve interacting with others on a violent level.

Different soldiers have different expectations; some look forward to combat while others freeze up at the first sign of conflict. This is not unusual and has happened throughout history. The human experience and reaction to conflict are very similar now to how they were back in Roman days, to give you a time perspective. The methodologies and techniques have changed, and weapons and schemes have become modernized, but the psyche of the soldier who goes off to war, leaving behind family and loved ones and coming face-to-face with his own mortality, has stayed the same.

When soldiers leave for war in a distant land, many are excited about the possible victory they will encounter. Others begin to miss their loved ones at home as their minds drift back to the safe confines of their comfortable habitats. All soldiers, before they go into battle, go through multiple exchanges in their emotions. Some are high on adrenaline, while others freeze with the thought of imminent attack. Some are happy to finally face the enemy they have waited so long for, which in itself was causing undue stress. The emotions can range from one horizon to the other and everything in between.

"We will tell them why things are the way they are. We don't cut corners—we speak the truth. We've been there, we understand the situation, and we know what you're going through."

Not all of us died in combat. Soldiers came home and struggled with the same feelings you're currently dealing with. But even those of us who came directly to this side can still feel your pain and the trauma that you deal with on a daily basis. We have put together a group of highly trained specialists who will be answering your questions and trying to explain to you in human terms why these things are the way they are.

It is our duty to help you relieve the pain that controls your life and the lives of the people around you. You do not have to accept every explanation we give you, but if you open your mind to the possibilities, you might be able to understand some of the reasons for what's happening to you in the situations around you.

Don't depend on us for all the answers; seek out your brothers and sisters, for they will have many ways of dealing with the physical and emotional pain. They are your immediate source of strength, and when they're not available, we are always here. We always hear your prayers, and we always try to intercede for you, but sometimes it is difficult with the current state of your psyche.

Do not be hesitant to ask for help. We will guide you in this process. You are not walking alone on this road. We walk next to you, by your side, in front of you, and we have your backs. You may not see us, feel us, or hear us, but that doesn't mean we're not here. Just because we are no longer living on your plane of existence does not mean we are not involved in your lives. We are brother veterans, and we stand with you in your triumph and in your grief.

In this book, we will concentrate on several levels of the problems that modern-day veterans are experiencing. It is important to realize that there are others involved in this learning experience, including family, friends of the veterans, and society in general. One's peace of mind is of the utmost importance to us.

We have been waiting for this opportunity to come forward and explain our position on living the daily life of the soldier. It's a simple thing: Do your job, get home safe. And that's our job now—to get you home safe. We know that even though some of you are at home, you really are not. **Part of you is still over there, and this is the part that we want to welcome home.**

Chapter 2

WHO I AM AND WHY I CHOSE TO WRITE THIS BOOK

My name is Joe Higgins. I am a Medium and Channeler. I have been given an extraordinary opportunity to communicate with those who have passed to the other side and have witnessed the connection and love that continue after the change we call death. In recent years, I have focused on channeling information from guides and teachers in order to bring this much-needed information to the Earth plane. I am humbled that during this life, I can make a difference in someone's life and perhaps even make a difference in the development of knowledge throughout the world.

At the end of the summer of 2012, I was reading some news online and came across an article about how some soldiers had recently been killed and others injured in Afghanistan. The thing that struck me the most is the fact that it wasn't a headline. It was one of many pieces of that particular day's news.

I also noticed continuing articles on service members returning home with disabilities and posttraumatic stress syndrome and how the number of people serving in the last 10 years and the number of suicides and mental health issues had risen sharply.

It struck me that the wars that we have been involved in for over a decade have seemed to become commonplace to most Americans. The fact that we still have soldiers risking their lives in conflict zones is something that the majority of people just file away on the back burner. While politicians fight over political causes and the masses are caught up in the daily entertainment fix, I thought it was necessary to do something to help our soldiers.

I didn't know how to bring this awareness to the forefront where it should be—on a national level—but I thought perhaps I could do something personally to help our troops and the families that support them. So I began to think about what I could do to help out. Could I volunteer to raise money, could I send more food to the troops overseas, or perhaps something different?

Over the last couple of years, during which time I've done a lot of writing, I learned many concepts related to how to focus one's life in order to achieve one's purpose. One of these concepts is *do what you do best*. Many of us have heard this statement before, and it came to me while thinking about what I could do to help our servicemen and women. Then I realized that what I do best is channel information from a higher realm. I've been able to bring forth knowledge on how signs are given from deceased loved ones in my first book, *Hello ... Anyone Home?*

So I thought it would bring comfort and healing if soldiers could get answers to some of the questions that are constantly on their minds about war in general as well as their personal involvement in it and the process of acclimating when they return home. I began to think that it would be especially powerful if this information came from fellow veterans who have passed to the other side, for what I have realized from my writings and my mediumship is that once we cross over, our perspective on our life here on the Earth plane is much different from how we see ourselves when we are living it. I realized that if veterans who have passed to the other side could relate back some common experiences that today's soldiers are dealing with, I could bring great insight and potential healing to those in need.

Transmitting information from veterans who have experienced the effects of war and conflict to today's veterans seemed like a powerful way to introduce this information. I thought it was extremely important for this information to come from veterans to veterans. I recognized the importance of those who have served in the capacity of soldier to be able to help fellow soldiers dealing with the same types of challenges in the present.

I was apprehensive about whether I could write such a book, fearful that I was stepping way out of my comfort zone, and unsure I would even be able to produce such a piece of work. I struggled for a few weeks in deciding if I would write this book. I had that nervous excitement that people can feel in their gut when they're ready to step into the unknown. While I was trying to rationalize why I couldn't write such a book, my spirit had already made the decision to move forward. Even though I tried to rationalize that being a non-veteran trying to write the book for veterans just wouldn't work, my inner spirit knew that the decision had already been made, that there was no turning back, and that this project needed to be completed.

Probably the biggest question I had was related to the fact that I had never served in the Armed Forces. I wondered how veterans and active soldiers could accept advice and information from someone who has not been directly involved in war or conflict. There would be no legitimacy. I thought I would be criticized and pushed to the side since I had no direct experience with the book's subject matter.

But then I realized that this book is not about me. It's not about how I feel, and it's not about my insecurity about being criticized or open to questions. If I were to be criticized, ignored, and belittled as someone giving guidance who has never actually been in a conflict situation, I would have to accept it because the bigger picture was about allowing this information through in hopes of bringing healing to those on this plane who desperately need it. If my simple fear of inadequacy was going to stop me from providing this information, I would be acting in a self-serving way, which would not be possible if I wished to continue to work with the spirit realm.

When I decided to begin the outline for the book, I realized that the information to be transferred was of such importance that nothing could hold me back from providing it. My selfish fears of inadequacy in the subject area would be put to the side for the greater good. In layman's terms, I told myself "suck it up—it's for the greater good."

While I was organizing my thoughts regarding the structure of the book and who I would be dealing with from the other side, arrangements were made about how the process would work. A group of guides and veterans who had passed to the other side would help me organize the questions and answers that we thought would help in the healing process of the soldiers and civilians of today.

One of the first things that came through, from a spokesman who would share information on behalf of the larger group, was about dealing with my insecurities about writing the book. The first thing they said was that the reason they had chosen me to bring forth this information was because I was a non-veteran. They explained to me that they needed someone who had no background or experience in war or a conflict zone in order to bring through the information without preconceived experiences corrupting it. They did not want my personal thoughts, experiences, or explanations to confuse the information coming directly from spirit. They believed that if I had been involved in war or conflict or had been a soldier at some time, I would have preconceived notions about how things should work or why they work as they do. By being a civilian without access to this type of information or experiences, it left me open to information that would be new to me to transcribe and present to those in need.

After receiving this information, I realized exactly how important it was that I was not a soldier. It made perfect sense to me that it would be difficult to write a book of this magnitude if I'd had my own experiences in a war zone.

Many civilians have had violent experiences that can cause posttraumatic stress syndrome. This syndrome is not solely a result of war. I, like many others, have experienced a time of posttraumatic stress syndrome.

Like many fellow Americans, I have interacted with friends and family who have served or who are currently serving in the Armed Forces. My father served in the Navy during World War

II, and my uncles also served in the military during times of conflict. My uncle Francis was killed in the battle of Iwo Jima. My sister has served in the military as well as my brother-in-law, who is currently serving our country in the Army.

I have always had a strong patriotic connection to veterans, possibly because growing up I was around many veterans who were friends with my father. I've also had classmates as well as coworkers and friends throughout my life who joined the military. I've always believed that the sacrifice one makes in joining the military is to be looked up to and admired. I've felt the same about the families of those who serve in the Armed Forces—that they are also to be looked up to and admired. Many people do not realize the fear of the unknown that resides within the civilians left at home when a loved one is called to serve.

So it is with utmost pride that I have been chosen to transcribe this information from veterans on the other side to our men and women who are currently serving in the Armed Forces and those who have served in conflict zones around the world. It is my intention to bring as much healing and understanding as possible in this area. Some people may understand parts of this book more than others, but it is written to individuals from individuals. My goal is to help those in need, and I have recruited the best helpers—those who have been there and experienced all aspects of war who have a larger perspective than any of us can see while living on the Earth plane.

I think it's important to remind people that this book does not cover all the questions we may have about war or all questions we may have about how to deal with traumatic events. It's not supposed to be the end-all as far as answers go. We all want answers to these questions wrapped up in neat packages with bows on top. But in real life, that's just not how things work. So my intention was to take some of the most frequently asked questions and try to get answers that might bring understanding and healing to those who read them. There were dozens and dozens of other questions I wanted to ask to obtain more knowledge, but that would have taken me in a different direction and changed the scope and focus of the book. I tried to keep the questions as relevant as possible so today's veterans might have something to work with.

I could have gone into more detail about how past conflicts and war related to particular cultures and civilizations, but that is not needed at this point. Down the line at some other time, perhaps, that is a path I can take. But for now I'm trying to make it as easy as possible for readers to understand concepts that may be directly affecting them today. I asked those involved to make the information easy to understand so as to be able to be used by the vast majority of readers.

This is not the holy grail of the answers to these complex questions. It is, however, insight into why these questions occur and how veterans of the past have dealt with them. Some of this book may be understandable for some and not others. As I was writing this book, I noticed that certain parts seem to focus on one particular group of veterans, while other parts seem to focus on a different area and time. I believe this was the intention of the guides and veterans that I've been channeling. They know where this book is supposed to go and who it is supposed to help. So while working together, I navigate the ship while they make decisions about content and purpose.

If people can take some parts of this book and use it to help in the healing process, it will have been a success. They don't need to accept or use all the information in order to achieve this milestone. Some will use certain parts of the book, while others will use other sections. Some will get the big picture, and some will focus in on only one or two pieces of information that will help them in their learning process.

Some will ask new questions about how things work, while others will begin to digest this knowledge that has been released to them. Much of this information may sound like old news. However, it may be that the deceased vets need to reinforce some of this information so people can focus in on it and use it to a higher degree. Many times we hear advice from others over and over, only to agree with it but not use it. How often does that happen in our lives? Our doctors tell us to eat healthy, but do we do it? We're told to relieve stress in our lives and are given examples of how to do it. But do we take that advice? Maybe we take some advice and forget the rest. Maybe we need to hear this advice and knowledge over and over before we take it to task. That may be the case with this book. Maybe it needs to be viewed from the context of veterans who have crossed over and who have a better perspective on how these traumas have affected our lives. Perhaps this new perspective of theirs provides a more legitimate foundation to some of the advice we have heard throughout our lives.

I would caution readers not to take these answers and pieces of knowledge lightly, for they have been thought out and were important enough to be transferred from the spiritual side of life to our current life on the Earth plane.

I understand that some veterans might be looking for some answers that they will not find in this book. Every veteran can gain knowledge and advice from aspects of this book, but it will not be everything to everybody.

So take the book for what it is—information channeled from the spirit world from veterans who have been in your position and who want to help you in the learning and healing process.

As a good friend of mine, DJ Harrington, likes to say to me (and I'm sure you've heard the expression before), it's like eating fish—eat the meat and spit out the bones. Take what you want from this book and use it, and just ponder the rest.

Chapter 3

WHO THEY ARE AND WHY THEY CHOSE TO WRITE THIS BOOK

Who They Are

Joe, we would like to introduce ourselves to your readers so they know where this information is coming from. We are a group of entities that have experienced life in human form on your plane. While we were in existence—that is, your physical existence—we experienced the trials and tribulations of mortal combat. You know us by the more common term of soldiers.

I will be speaking for the group of us who have had experiences that we will be talking about throughout the book. This way, you will not be distracted by different voices and will be able to choose and transcribe the information much more easily and quickly.

We come from all branches of life. Some of us were farmers, and others were industrialists. We flew planes, drove tanks, and fought hand-to-hand, and some were station on the seas. When it comes to veterans, their experiences, and what they're going through, we have a unique perspective because we have gone through it ourselves while living on your plane of existence. We had those same doubts, the same feelings of stress, and the uncontrollable urges that some of you are experiencing today. Some of us were killed in action, while others were dismembered and had horrific disabilities before we passed over.

So we experienced many of the same sights, sounds, and smells that you may have in combat. Others who never saw combat had the same experiences as modern-day soldiers who have not seen combat but who feel a camaraderie with their fellow soldiers. These soldiers grapple with unique questions such as, "Why wasn't I chosen to be in a situation of life and death? How can I talk to a veteran who comes back from a combat mission that I've never experienced? Am I less of a soldier and less of a veteran if I did not see hand-to-hand combat and wasn't involved in the launching of missiles or the dropping of bombs?" The deceased veterans in our group have insights and help for those who experience similar quandaries today.

For the purpose of this book, we will tap into individuals for their stories of the experiences they had while in combat. For general questions and answers, we as a group will try to answer them for your readers. It is our experience that we will have an effect on the people who read this book, so we will be careful not to release information that may be harmful to others. By harmful, we mean information that may bring unease and suffering since our job is to relieve suffering and bring healing. We are acutely aware of this obligation, and we will keep an eye on it for you.

We will offer you a series of statements that you will be able to transcribe for us and share with veterans who need this information to make sense of their current lives. We will answer questions that we have put forth that are common to veterans of all ages concerning our role and their role in conflict.

We hope to be able to explain the different scenarios and actions that were taken and the reasons they occurred. Many times our reactions and actions were taken with very little knowledge of the situation at hand, but being on the other side now, we are able to put things in perspective and see the reasons that certain actions were taken.

We remain focused on helping our fellow veterans achieve prosperous and healing lives and helping them understand what they have experienced.

Joe, we realize this is not an easy subject for you and that you are a third party transcribing the information from us to them. We realize that you have apprehension about the subject since you are not a veteran yourself. We sought someone out with your abilities so it would not interfere with personal experiences. Your experiences cannot color our information because you have not experienced them yourself.

This gives us an advantage in that we don't have to work through barriers that have already been set up in a veteran's psyche. By working through you, Joe, not only do we have a fantastic communicator but also someone who is not jaded or holding preconceived answers to questions that current veterans have.

We have been waiting for an opportunity to bring this information to humanity, as so many have questions and concerns when it comes to the conflicts between each other on your plane of existence. Why do people kill? Why do people treat others as they do? Why do I have to suffer by interceding in these conflicts? These are questions that all soldiers asked themselves.

Unfortunately, many soldiers carry these questions and burdens throughout their lives. We are here to relieve them of these burdens by explaining the process by which events take place. We hope to guide current veterans in the healing process as they return home to reinstate their lives and put into perspective the experiences they have witnessed and participated in.

We have no judgment about the actions or interpretations that veterans have about themselves or how they see their fellow brothers in action.

For as you will see, no judgment is necessary—things happen for a reason—but we hope to explain some of these reasons. We also want to make veterans aware of who they really are: spiritual beings. As is often seen in combat, the physical body interacts with the spiritual essence of who you really are, and this in itself can cause reactions that are not always comfortable for the individual soldier.

We have all experienced the horrors, the complex and glorious triumphs, and the disappointments of war as well as regional conflicts. Our experiences are not unusual; it is only the techniques carried out that have changed over the years.

The interactions between family, friends, civilians, and home life are actually quite similar throughout the ages from the perspective of the soldier. We can understand the problems with reconnecting as well as the burden of having our lives change forever yet wanting to get our lives back to the way they were. We realize the problems that current soldiers are suffering and that the injuries are not just physical but can be emotional, intellectual, and spiritual as well. We will work on all these levels, for it is our understanding that many people currently returning home from war are realizing that something has changed within them, and they are now open to seeking information and knowledge from our side.

In the past, we would come to individual veterans and try to bring them healing through their dreams as well as by working through others such as counselors and healers on your plane. But we relish the thought of coming to veterans through a medium who can transcribe and share our words and hopefully bring healing, understanding, and knowledge to a vast number of people all at once.

We hope that by doing this, we are also able to help future veterans returning from conflicts as well as help the general population understand what veterans go through before, during, and after their involvement in a conflict.

We will explain certain types of conflict and how an individual soldier feels about getting involved in the action. By this, we mean that if there's a physical attack on one's home or area of living, the reaction is slightly different than if one must travel a great distance in order to fight an enemy whom the soldier does not know or perhaps even see. These different complexities bring up different questions that we will also try to address.

We would also like to touch base regarding the leaders in some of these circumstances. Certain leaders bring additional concerns to us about having to lead others into conflict because they know they will be responsible for these young soldiers. Some of these officers carry a great burden upon returning home, knowing that some of the decisions they made cost the lives of some soldiers and caused physical trauma to others. Their so-called curse can be well hidden from fellow soldiers, as they believe they have a higher responsibility not to show the vulnerability that others may be allowed.

Our involvement in this book has been brought about as we seek to bring this information from our side to your side. We want to give you answers and help the healing process from one veteran to another veteran, from people who would have been there and seen similar things that you have experienced but who also have the perspective of seeing and experiencing the situation from the Other Side.

You see, from our side, a lot of things make sense. We might not have all the answers, but we can help you put your lives in order or at least give you the tools to understand the process of war and conflict.

With these new tools, understanding, and knowledge, you will be able to create your future the way it was meant to be. Some had access to this knowledge in earlier conflicts, but today large numbers of soldiers are returning who lack the ability to make that connection. At times it's just the sheer number of soldiers who need this knowledge, and at other times the impetus comes from our desire to bring this knowledge to your plane of existence.

We will try not to get too complex with our explanations, as at times we may cross over into a more philosophical discussion. We will try to make it, as Joe says, an "easy read" so more people have access to the information and will continue to use some of the ideas and explanations that we give to him for the benefit of all.

Right now we are gathering our forces in order to work on this project. Many, many veterans are involved in the information that we will bring to you. We have been working on this for some time, and we relish the opportunity to bring it forward now. You will be given information from many different sides and conflicts. At times you will get insight into the minds and feelings of others whom you may have labeled as the enemy.

Soldiers are soldiers, and, depending on the conflict and the culture, will go through different phases of reactivation when returning home. But there are many common themes with any type of soldier, such as losing friends in combat and witnessing horrible things that you wish you never saw. The sounds, the smells, the sights of various conflicts are common among all soldiers who participated in a particular conflict, no matter which side of the battlefield they stood on.

Why They Chose to Write This Book
Joe, the reason we chose to write this book is that, for too long, people have misunderstood our connection to your plane. Through the information we pass along through you, we hope to bring relief from the suffering of millions of people who have been directly and indirectly affected by conflict and war. Some of these people had their lives changed for the better and others for the worse. Many of these people are soldiers in arms. These people suffer on a daily basis, and many times the treatment they must seek out does not answer the questions that burden them every day.

The reason we use veterans on our side to reach the veterans on your side is because of the bonding that veterans associate with each other. They are more apt to use the information that we provide to you if they realize that it is coming from veterans who have experienced the same things they are experiencing right now.

Joe, you will facilitate the bringing of information in order to relieve the suffering of many of these people who do not have hope. Your efforts will assist us in assisting veterans in overcoming obstacles that are holding them back from their growth during this lifetime. You will give them many tools that they can use to relieve some of the mental anxiety as they search for answers. Soldiers will use these techniques to get their lives in order and to be able to enjoy the opportunities that life offers them.

Once we have arrived on the other side and have seen how our experiences in war have affected our beings, we become very humble, knowing that we had put undue stress, guilt, and judgment upon ourselves. Although this was unnecessary at the time, it was part of being a veteran or active soldier in the middle of conflict. But now, being on the other side, we can see that we put ourselves on pedestals to be judged, and we ourselves were our harshest judges. Realizing this is one of the main reasons we wanted to write this book. We wanted to let today's veterans realize that their actions or inactions are not to be judged on a personal basis.

Once you arrive in a physical existence on Earth, many of the tools and lessons that you have brought with you are put aside and not utilized. We will discuss some of these in the book. Some people may be aware of these tools, such as your intuition, gut feelings, and the ability to sense certain situations.

However, oftentimes you do not tap into these resources or utilize them in the way in which they were intended. You have a system of checks and balances within your body that regulates your physical being. When the body becomes out of balance, it creates certain symptoms for which a course of treatment is to be taken. A well-regulated human body can carry you throughout your life in order to learn and experience lessons that you have come to participate in.

What is often forgotten is the true essence of one's self and how it is integrated into the human physical experience. The spiritual entity that makes up the true you is the essence that drives your experiences. This spirit is a combination of past experiences, knowledge, expectations, and realizations. It has the ability to change the energy around others as well as the power to heal and comfort others of the same makeup.

Spiritual awareness is extremely important to the process of learning and experiencing on your plane. Your true spiritual essence is your compass, which you must follow in order to complete the lessons that you have agreed to participate in. Some people are very aware of the lessons and experiences they have to learn and go about them in a timely manner. Others fluctuate between different directions and different opportunities, not knowing which to take advantage of and which to dismiss.

What we wish for you to realize is that this inner compass that you have access to is all that you need to rely on to find the correct course that your life is meant to follow. As with any journey, there will always be course corrections and abrupt changes. This is part of the adventure of the human existence. You will surely not see a journey start at one point and go straight to another point, for this would be a very short experience and would not give you the opportunity to learn the wonders and experiences that are only available on your physical plane.

Short journeys of existence are initiated for the purpose of helping others. People who only lived for a short period of time have accepted this assignment in order to teach others about love and compassion. They have given up a great opportunity to have new experiences in order to bring an opportunity to others. The loss of children is a prime example of this type of sacrifice. Many times people wonder why God has taken a peaceful and special child when there are so many so-called evil people allowed to live for a longer time. These children have made an exemplary sacrifice in order to help others in their learning process.

We realize that it is difficult for parents and loved ones who have lost a child or others who have lost seemingly innocent loved ones. What we want you to know is that their passing was intentional and that they themselves had orchestrated it in order for you and others to appreciate love and find hope in the mist of despair, anger, and fear. These loved ones, even though only on the Earth plane for a short period of time, can create immensely powerful lessons for those left behind. It is a part of existence that few will take part in because of the extreme emotional results that can take place.

Others have decided to live much longer lives. These people will also contribute to the learning and the experiences of others. For in the length of their time on the Earth plane, they will come in contact with many situations and people with whom they will be able to interact and influence in a positive manner. As the body begins to age and break down, new experiences will begin to reveal themselves to the person and all that's around them. This is also a difficult road to take for some, as age can be complicated, physically painful, and filled with many obstacles. People who choose this particular path realize that they will have the opportunity for many more learning experiences.

Everyone who has come to the Earth plane has made a decision to interact with others on various levels. These levels can be physical, emotional, and spiritual. Each soul will have the opportunity to learn things for themselves as well as the opportunity to provide others with learning experiences.

These same learning experiences can come about in vastly different ways. One's life does not have to stay on a certain path in order for one to complete the journey. Many different roads lead to the acquisition of the lessons and knowledge one has come to this plane to gain. The interactions between different souls can at times be violent and uncomfortable. These too are part of the learning experience. So it is important to realize that there are many ways to learn your life lessons. At times, others' interactions with you may be planned for the purpose of your growth. At other times, the interactions may be planned for their growth. There are also times when an interaction between two individuals will occur for the growth of a larger group, for at times individual souls are needed to help teach a larger group and expand their ability to grow and experience life as a collective.

This is where the existence of the individual and the existence of a group come together. On an individual basis, you will learn lessons and have experiences. You will also have the ability to teach others and be a part of their lessons. But there is also a third aspect of your existence on the Earth plane: the group.

The group setting is an important part of existence on the Earth plane, as it is made up of individual souls working together, interacting, and by doing so, creating lessons and experiences for the group as a whole. When the power of awareness, love, and compassion is experienced by many individuals, it will continue on a larger scale within a group. This is how nations and cultures move forward in their growth and understanding of the human experience. As you participate in one of these groups, it gives you another opportunity to learn and experience the higher levels of enlightenment.

In order for these individuals and groups to grow, they will experience opportunities that will cause them concern. Being involved in war and violent conflict is one of these. Individuals come into larger conflicts with different sets of understanding and knowledge. Their beliefs and level of development will be different from others who share the same experiences.

War is a group effort, and it brings about immense learning opportunities. It is difficult for some to understand this concept, especially those who are directly involved in the violent nature of this interaction. Those who have witnessed the cruelty that some humans inflict on others can have their internal compass—their moral ground—shaken to the core of their essence.

That is why this book is so important—to help them realize that they are part of a larger picture and that they as individuals are part of a greater learning experience for both themselves and others.

Chapter 4

THE PROCESS AND TRANSFER OF KNOWLEDGE

We seek out mediums and channelers in order to transfer information to your plane of existence. We need you to help us transfer this knowledge. We have other methods of interacting with your side, but at times it is easier to work through an individual, so Joe has been chosen to be a part of this transfer of knowledge. When more detailed information and knowledge need to be transferred, we accept the fact that an individual is at times the best medium or way to accomplish this goal.

The transfer of knowledge has been going on since the beginning of time. We work with individuals one-on-one but also work on larger subjects concerning many people, societies, and cultures. When people ask us questions, we try to give them legitimate answers. Information is not always allowed to be transferred due to the circumstances around the releasing of that knowledge.

If all information were released to you on your plane of existence, many of the lessons you came here for would not be able to be accomplished. You would understand the concept of this information, but you would not have the ability to experience it firsthand. It is one thing to learn something through the transfer of knowledge from one to another, and another thing altogether to learn it through experience.

Some may say that holding back this knowledge is wrong and that to do so causes much pain and suffering. This is not the reason this information is kept back. Your existence is specifically designed for experiencing things firsthand. Your potential growth would be stunted if this information were just handed to you. You see, the ultimate goal is to achieve this knowledge through firsthand experience and to be able to learn from it and grow at a spiritual level.

Then why is this information allowed to come through? you may ask. Because at times this information is needed in order to understand the experiences that you are going through. These experiences are often of such magnitude that they can corrupt the learning and understanding of the experience. This can also corrupt the learning experience to the degree that the reason the person's existence in the first place is not in line with the growth that has taken place. For example, a soldier's experience may be so traumatic that his ability to understand it is compromised and new learning is stopped. Many may not understand this concept, but it is important to remember that *just because you have the knowledge does not mean you have the understanding.*

So at times throughout history, we have contacted a few who have the ability to transfer this knowledge to the masses. We have the ability to do it on an individual basis, such as through creativity and prayer, in order to help people understand the meaning of life. At other times, we enjoy bringing through explanations and understanding of how the process of life works. Some concepts and explanations will never be received in the way they are meant, and therefore they are held back. Once you are reunited on the spiritual side of existence, you will understand this concept.

Some may be afraid to accept this information, while others may consider it to be false. Those who wish to downplay this information have a concern that it may come from a source that is not of the highest moral and ethical makeup. This is understandable, as information has been transferred from other entities that are not looking out for the best of humanity. They may wish to cause chaos and suffering through misinformation and the corruption of the process for their own personal, selfish, and ignorant reasons. They may also wish to pass on information that will serve their own purposes in order to gain strength on your plane of existence. We understand that many people have different names for these types of entities and interactions, but they all have certain things in common. They bring uncertainty, harm, misunderstanding, and fear. These are signs that the information coming through is not necessarily from a higher order of existence.

However, many times the information that comes through is from a higher order of existence and is intended to help humanity understand the experiences they are learning at this time. Those who fear this information are apt to have to recreate experiences over and over through many lives before accepting the knowledge that was presented to them at a previous time. An example of this may be a person who is learning how to swim. When he goes near water, he will touch the water, go in up to his knees, and then come out. This can go on for years, in contrast to the person who will learn how to swim in just one summer. Others may not accept this information due to the fact that they are still trying to comprehend other information that has been passed along to them. This early information has not been fully analyzed and understood at a soul level, and they are not prepared to accept new information on top of it. They become conflicted regarding accepting some pieces of information and not others. Once you start to break up this knowledge in that particular way, it can become confusing and unreliable.

So our goal is to bring this information to as many people as possible and let each individual make his own choice as to the level of acceptance that he is comfortable with in order to use this knowledge to grow and understand his spiritual path.

This knowledge we seek to pass over to you will cover many subjects and experiences in a human's life experiences. Some may be personal and spiritual, while others may be about how societies have developed and the particulars of the makeup and abilities of humans and the structures they lived in. Some may understand this under the term *science*.

We understand that there are many cultural and religious differences between souls on the Earth plane. We will not discuss that in great depth in this book because we believe that that information will take away attention that needs to be focused on the subject we are discussing. At times we will comment on a particular culture or religion as it relates to the condition of the soldier, his family, and the community to which he belongs. We realize that war and conflict are often intertwined with religious and cultural differences.

This can be understood, as larger groups are experiencing the fear and misunderstanding of the information that we have passed along throughout the ages. As we mentioned earlier, some individuals may not be able to process this information and as such may cause larger groups or communities to take this route to war and conflict. Some have described it as more enlightened cultures versus cultures that wish to remain stagnant. This may be the case from a certain perspective, but it does not cover the understanding of the total process of accumulating knowledge and experiences. Sometimes those cultures are needed in order to learn and experience growth.

If all people in all cultures were at the same level of development, it would be very difficult for individuals to move along the spiritual path and grow without having firsthand opportunities presented to them. Yes, there is a duality to life on the Earth plane. Some explain it by saying you cannot have good without evil, you cannot have compassion without suffering, you cannot have insight without ignorance. This is true to a certain extent; it gives you a scale or a base in order to see where you are in the learning process.

Once you have crossed over and back to your original spiritual essence, you will see the experiences you have had with a different perspective. You will see the part you played in your own development as well as the part you played in the development of others. Some may be limited to individual participation between souls, while others' participation might be on a larger scale, dealing with millions of souls at the same time. No matter which, your interaction with others will be the source of your learning and knowledge.

We ask that this information that is coming through be used for the peaceful transition of the human experience and to bring about an awareness of the process of growth. We wish people to understand that our interaction with your side is brought about as a natural process of guiding people on their path. It's like a parent guiding a child in learning new experiences.

You are individual souls who are on a journey to increase your knowledge of life. By increasing this knowledge and understanding this information, a soul can progress to a higher state of enlightenment. As more learning experiences take place and more information is acquired, your ability to pass on this information to others will be allowed. So you are not only growing for yourself, you are growing in order to help others. You all are learning to become teachers, but you must first pass the courses of life on the Earth plane.

Chapter 5
PHYSICAL SOLDIER/SPIRITUAL BEING

Joe, we have been asked many times who we actually are, meaning who we are as people. The simple answer that most people have is the physical body, the experiences that make up their lives, and the dreams and hopes they have for themselves and their families. These are all true on a certain level. But once you pass over, you have a larger perspective on the existence that you just lived. We can see the "whys" and the "hows" and the "whens," and we can see how individuals interact with other individuals. We can see this on an everyday basis, we can feel the emotions that people feel, and we can feel the stress as well as the hopes and dreams and love and laughter that people experience.

You see, you are not only a physical being made up of bone, blood, and organs—you are actually a spiritual being made up of all your thoughts, desires, hopes, and a multitude of other parts that we will not go into right now. When your spiritual being takes form in a physical body, certain actions and reactions take place that need to coincide in order for there to be balance. If this balance is disrupted to a certain degree, the experience on your plane can become overburdened, and some may become stressful and painful. If your physical body and your spiritual body are not in alignment, physical manifestations can occur. We see this in stress, depression, and unhappiness as well as in many physical expressions, from aches and pains to being unable to focus to the physical deterioration of the body.

When a soldier goes to war, many times this alignment is thrown out of balance very quickly and very acutely. It's like being on a seesaw and you're in the air, and your partner quickly steps off and you come crashing to the ground. There is a shift in that balance between your spiritual body, your spiritual self, and your human existence. We can see this from our side. It is the major contributing factor in the experiences that some veterans have before, during, and after involvement in a conflict.

While your physical body and mind are reacting to orders, learned in training , that you have received to carry out a certain mission—to perhaps have to kill another human being or manipulate certain situations in order to create an advantage for your side—your spirit, which is the true you, tries to acclimate to the situation. But your spirit cannot totally acclimate to the experiences that you are currently having. You are a caring, loving being, and you've come here to learn lessons that can only be experienced on this physical plane. When you are in a conflict zone, your true self is put at odds with the physical being that you inhabit on this plane.

When you ask yourself how you could have done certain things that you did and how people can treat each other in such a way, it seems unearthly, like chaos or a description of hell. And you cannot understand these aspects because your true spiritual body is not made up of them—you are of a higher existence than these lower-level experiences.

Some ask, "Then why are we allowed to experience these events?" The answer is because many of you will learn lessons and grow from these events, which will actually make you become a better, more highly evolved spirit.

For example, you may be put in a position in which you save someone's life. You may put your own life on the line in order to prevent the death or disability of a fellow human. That in itself is a huge learning experience. You may feel guilty about some of the things that you have done, but there are also lessons built into those experiences. We do not wish for you to overanalyze every situation you are in to see if the lesson to be learned was acquired. One of the symptoms of being in a war situation is the recurring events that take place after the original event has already transpired. You may call it "soul searching" or "reliving the past." It's all just another form of self-judgment.

The missions you went on and the things you were trained for were all part of lessons to be learned during your lifetime on this physical plane. Your inability to deal with these experiences is not your fault—it is your spiritual body trying to come to terms with experiences that are a lower form of learning.

Some veterans may ask what someone can learn if they are killed in action. What they will learn is when they get to our side they will see the cause-and-effect of what they have done and how it has related to those around them. Their passing will come as lessons to loved ones and friends and fellow soldiers. This death will create more thought and self-judging by many others and this we want to stop.

If a commander sends soldiers into battle and some are killed or maimed because of his decision, he might rethink that decision for many years to come. His analytical brain may wear on him and the decisions he made in that time frame. But he does not know what actions may have occurred if he had not made that decision—what lessons and opportunities for learning might have been lost. He has no sight into the future or how things could have changed. As the saying goes, "That is way higher than his pay grade."

So you are a spiritual being who has chosen to take on the physical attributes of a soldier during your life on the Earth plane. Realizing this will open the door to many wonderful insights and abilities that you will be able to tap into in order to heal yourself and help others. Do not doubt this, for this is the most powerful tool of them all—the awareness of who you really are.

PART II

Chapter 6
WHY IS WAR NECESSARY?

The concept of war is an intriguing subject to many people in all cultures around the world. Since the beginning of time, there has always been interaction between different peoples in different geographic locations around the globe. War at its basic source is conflict between two opposing positions that has reached a stage of violent interaction. By this, we mean opposing ideas have not been able to be worked out between individuals and groups and have escalated to the point at which physical interaction is necessary to complete an outcome.

War can be confined to a small geographical area or occur between nations on many continents at the same time. War throughout time has been instigated for many reasons; we will touch upon just a few. The root cause comes down to individuals' lack of understanding of how to deal with issues of the day.

There are times when individuals wish to push their individual concepts onto the masses and to control others in particular ways that are only seen through the leaders' eyes. In this example, we can see certain individuals throughout time who created chaos in the expansion of their powers through the use of conflict and war. There has been no righteous concern or thought behind these conflicts but one of selfishness—the seeking of power, control, and manipulation of people and cultures. From a spiritual perspective, we see it as individuals grouping together under a common theme to act upon a common approach to acquire control.

When a soul comes to the Earth plane, he arrives in order to learn lessons that will help his soul progress to a higher stage of enlightenment. This enlightenment can be judged by certain common traits, such as compassion, the ability to love, and the ability to have empathy and understanding of others in their quest for learning.

All spiritual beings who exist on the physical plane are at different levels of development, and their interactions with one another sometimes come into conflict. If an entity at a lower form of development is in a position of leadership or control, he can move a group more easily into a conflict situation than ones who have learned certain lessons and acquired higher skills.

As humans continue to develop on the physical plane in their growth as spiritual beings, there will always be aspects of conflict, some of which will lead to violence. Some of the primal instincts that humans possess in order to survive on the physical plane are tapped into and used incorrectly when resolutions of disputes cannot be worked out.

Many times individuals' particular beliefs about the reasons for their lives and their purpose for being are in conflict with the beliefs of other groups of individuals. Some people believe so strongly in a cause that they are willing to extinguish their own life in order to inflict change on the situation they believe is of great importance. Some have honorable ideas and concepts, while others are determined to destroy certain other beliefs and cultures because they do not understand them and believe that those beliefs and cultures are a threat to their own.

As civilizations have developed throughout the ages, people and cultures have begun to understand that their involvement with other cultures must be looked at with responsibility for their actions. People of today realize they are accountable and responsible for their individual actions and therefore try to avoid conflict and war more often than in the past. People at national and international levels realize that certain basic human rights need to be upheld by all. Most nations and people realize that certain segments of our societies should not be overburdened with suffering and abuse. Even though the situations do still occur, the majority of the nations and people on the Earth plane are against these types of actions. An example of this is the killing of children during war and conflict in order to gain advantage over one's adversary. Another example is the use of children as warriors in order to gain emotional and psychological advantages within one's own military structure and culture. The treatment of individuals who are captured and held prisoner during conflict or war has come with responsibilities in a code of ethics by the capturing force. Many nations understand that the treatment of injured soldiers and the capture of enemy combatants must have a certain standard of human rights.

However, we continue to see that these lines of responsibility and accountability are crossed on a daily basis throughout the world. Some groups' cultures and nations are ruled by individuals who dismiss the idea of human rights toward one's adversaries. Their belief is that the strong have the right to inflict suffering and damage in any manner necessary in order to achieve their own goals.

This is where individuals' soul development comes in conflict with the growth of the culture or the nation. Nations and cultures also grow depending on the growth of their populations, meaning that the people who live in the geographical area or culture have a similar belief and grow as a group, depending on the individual soul growth of each member of that group. So as more individuals grow and learn the higher elements of compassion, love, understanding, and the ability to work with one another, their group, nation, or organization will also grow and be of more value to all the people of the world.

Some people may misunderstand this as a sign of weakness and not being able to engage in a conflict or a war situation. This is not the idea at all. Nations and groups that have continued to develop in a positive way can still, and often do, engage in the concept of war. Their reasons, however, are different from those of other groups, who may possess a limited ability in the area of love and compassion in their interactions with others. Many times these groups lash out in fear, just as we see on an individual basis.

As the development of individual souls continues on a planetary scale, there will always be conflict due to the different levels attained by individuals and nations. Some individuals may learn and become more enlightened, while others may stagnate or even regress in their development. There are certain individuals on the Earth plane who do not have the tools to understand the developmental process of their own souls. Their energy in essence is made up of conflicting emotions in different levels of development. They are not of their own but manifested from groups of emotions and primal fears and are made up of different parts of individual souls who have passed over before them.

There are entities who will manifest on the Earth plane whose only reason for existence is to cause chaos and disruption among the learning process of the souls who have come here to learn the higher levels of spiritual enlightenment. These individuals create chaos in others' lives and do not recognize any compassion, love, or enlightenment toward themselves or others. These entities actually enjoy inflicting suffering and mayhem on as many people as possible through their life experiences. An example of this might be people who are guilty of great crimes against humanity. This is not to be confused with individuals who have been involved in horrendous acts due to mental illness, stresses, or environmental conditions. These individuals are not on the same path of achieving enlightenment and growth that the majority of the souls on the Earth plane have chosen.

We do not want to go off the path of having you understand why war is at times necessary by bringing in other aspects of the spirit world. It is just a subject that needs to be mentioned, as some have wondered about the actions of some individuals throughout time. It is more important to understand the realities of why nations continue to inflict pain and suffering on others when, as individuals, we realize that this type of action is not always necessary. However, at times part of the learning process is to be involved in a conflict or war in order to protect the rights of human beings. It is difficult for individuals to sit and watch as other individuals are made to suffer for non-legitimate means.

However, these emotions can be used against individuals and nations in order to bring groups into conflict. Individuals and groups can manipulate national pride in order to gain legitimacy in the quest for war. Throughout time, certain individuals have been able to utilize the emotions of individuals in order to get large groups to follow them into and support them in conflict and war.

We ask that the peoples of the Earth plane realize that this takes place at times and to be vigilant to call these individuals on these actions. There are various reasons outside a difference of opinion as to why war begins. For example, the economic advantage of one group over another group can be a basis for the introduction of conflict and war.

We all have a responsibility to help each other in our development in learning the higher aspects of existence. Many of us learn this in an environment in which our senses and understanding are tested on a daily basis. However, with the idea of growing and becoming more compassionate and loving individuals, we can strive through the difficult times and situations that we face in our daily lives. Some lessons of great importance will be found in the confines of war and conflict, as these may bring about opportunities for an individual to learn the concepts of a higher state of enlightenment. An example is in helping a fellow soldier or loved one who has problems accepting certain situations in life. As an individual, it is important to find that opportunity within a chaotic situation to learn and help others learn higher and more positive lessons.

Chapter 7

WHY DO HUMANS TREAT EACH OTHER IN SUCH VIOLENT AND INDISCRIMINATE WAYS?

Since the beginning of time, humans have interacted with each other in violent ways in order to secure their position for safety and sustenance. As man has developed his spiritual being and new levels of consciousness have been reached, it is not necessary to have the survival techniques that early humans needed in the past. Many of the survival mechanisms have been hardwired into the human body so as not to be forgotten from one generation to another. People have always learned that safety was more easily acquired while in groups and thus started to create communities.

As time went on, these communities grew into cultures and nation states. As individuals rose among the ranks of leadership, they brought with them their own ideals and faults in leading these groups to interact with other groups in a violent way.

For it is easier to engage in violent behavior toward another while in a group. One's personal inner compass of right and wrong can be shifted when an individual is among others. What one person would never consider doing to another can change when that person is introduced into a group that is then placed in a situation in which violence will take place. The individual will inflict pain and suffering on another in order to achieve the goals of the group. This is the beginning of the turmoil that the individual will later relive and question at a spiritual level.

Some individuals, because of their inability to grow and understand as spiritual beings, will continue to inflict harm and chaos on others regardless of whether or not they are involved with a group. They have not grown to a level of understanding that the interaction between two individuals does not have to take place in a violent way. To these individuals, violence becomes a means to their particular end.

If these individuals are put in leadership positions at any level of a group, this will cause others to follow in this direction and be involved in violence that they normally would not have tolerated.

Once individuals are placed inside a war or conflict zone, especially when there with a group, their sense of right and wrong will be twisted and complicated by what they are observing and being forced to accept. These individuals may be trained to commit certain levels of violence in order to complete a specific mission. If this specific mission is backed up by a sense of security, justice, and moral righteousness, it will add to the individual's acceptance of creating this violence and disregard for fellow human beings.

So we see individuals at all different levels of learning interacting with one another in group situations, and this can cause a complex moral dilemma for some, while others will relish the ability to control and subjugate other humans.

Once an individual returns to the safety of his homeland and tries to acclimate back into the civilian world, parts of this individual are still controlled by the situations that have occurred in the conflict zone. Their interactions with others, which may have been reinforced by their interaction at a violent level with other humans, can start to cause great dismay once they start to analyze their actions.

All humans still have basic survival tendencies within their makeup. Many have seen this ability at some time in their life, either through the observations of others or perhaps their own involvement. The observation of these basic survival tendencies toward other human beings is analyzed and judged by the individual. Many will realize that these tendencies are not needed to the extent they might have been needed in earlier times. They realize that the violence that was once part of the survival process is no longer necessary. With this acceptance and realization, they continue on with their spiritual growth in learning new lessons from new opportunities.

Others will look at their actions and deem them to be appropriate for a particular situation. Some will reassure themselves that the violence they create is appropriate, and what they have instigated is the right thing to do. They miss the opportunity to realize that their basic instincts for survival have moved past the level of violent interaction in an indiscriminate way.

There are also some individuals whose spiritual makeup has been corrupted by other influences from the spiritual realm. These people have not moved up spiritually from a basic level. They may also be spiritual beings who are immature and mutant in their ability to ever develop to a higher level. These entities are constantly interacting with others, creating learning opportunities for others who are tested in their interactions with them.

These people may have similar characteristics, such as a lack of consciousness regarding their actions against fellow human beings. Some will even enjoy the chaos they bring about on the Earth plane. They are energized by the fear and anxiety they create, and they look for situations in which they can act upon these fears to feed their corrupt spirits.

These individuals are not to be confused with individuals who have developed mental conditions that may cause them to act out with violent and indiscriminate behaviors. The human body is a well-balanced chemical machine that at times may become out of sync. When this happens, an individual will have physical or emotional shifts from his normal spiritual abilities.

There are various causes for this disruption in the physical and mental conditions of individuals, but their interactions with others in violent and indiscriminate ways are not based on this spiritual level of development. Their system on the whole is broken, but they continue to live life as they think they should. Many times assistance is available to these individuals in order to bring the body back in balance. The ability of the individual to interact with others in order to bring this balance back depends on the individual's surrounding community. Some individuals in some geographic locations may not have the assistance that other individuals have access to. Some cultures may treat some of these conditions different than other cultures, and varying results can take place, depending on the techniques that are used.

Despair and depression can be the result of individuals interacting in violent and indiscriminate ways. These can be dealt with at various levels by the intervention of fellow human beings who wish to bring healing and peace to the affected individual.

It is important to remember that some individuals do not understand why they are acting out in the manner in which they have chosen. Some do not realize that help is available to assist them in bringing peace to their minds and bodies. It is up to the community where this individual resides to support this person and work with him in the most compassionate way possible. Individuals who have been through trauma need the assistance of others to reinforce that what they have experienced has shifted the balance within the body. Many people need to understand that individuals are going through this process, that it could be complex at times, and that these individuals need help in order to return to normal living.

Some people think there is an easy fix for people who developed difficulties after being involved in traumatic situations. This is not always the situation. It is important for people to realize that a quick fix might work for one but not work for many others. Each individual will have specific challenges and specific results, depending on the makeup of his being.

Social stigmas concerning mental illness are based on fear and misunderstanding of how the human body works. One's treatment should not be based upon such unreliable fear and anxiety. Awareness of how the human body has transcended through trauma and how to bring the body back into balance is what is truly important.

Chapter 8

I'M AFRAID THAT WHAT I'VE DONE HAS CHANGED ME

When one decides to become involved in a conflict zone, the process of self-realization as to the purpose of this decision begins. Many times, soldiers are conscripted into service without their approval and must engage in violent interactions with others. The self-analysis process can be different than it is for those who voluntarily decide to become involved in a conflict as well as for those who are pushed into the position, even though they do not wish to be involved.

When one volunteers and is put in the position of being intimate within a conflict, the self-analysis of that person's decision-making process is brought to a head. If forced into fighting, the soldier will focus on his lack of control over his own being. He will search for answers concerning the fact that others have taken control of his life and have put him in a situation of fear and turmoil.

Both types of soldiers—no matter which way they become involved in the conflict—will experience traumas and other situations that will alter who they believe they are. They will come into the conflict believing that they are a certain type of person and will exit the conflict with a different perspective.

Some will naturally grow through their experiences and become more mature, while others will be overwhelmed with the trauma they have witnessed and inflicted on others. As with any new experience, growth will be experienced, but during times of war and violent interaction, these new experiences will take on a higher degree of understanding. Soldiers will look deep inside themselves and begin to judge themselves on how they performed during their time of service. Some will learn that their only priority was survival, while others will appreciate the fact that they were involved in a situation in which they have been useful to the purpose of that particular cause. Some will be proud of the time they served, while others will wish to forget some of the experiences they were forced to be involved in.

Each individual soldier will grow as a person, regardless of the experience that each individual has been involved in. Growth can be understood as an acceptance of the new learning experience. While some may accept the awareness of these experiences, others will try to forget or suppress them. Those who wish to forget or suppress the experiences they have witnessed or been involved in will ultimately accept these new learning experiences on a subconscious level. This is where conflict will begin within many soldiers, and they will have trouble transitioning back into civilian life.

Some experiences may be judged and explored on different levels and thus take on different importance to the soldiers. They may wish to enhance certain experiences while subduing others. But all experiences will shape the change that the soldiers will find within themselves at the end of the conflict period. Many realize that once they enter into a conflict zone or participate in a war, the experiences they witness or were involved in will change them to a certain degree. However, many do not realize that the changes involved will be on multiple levels, such as emotional, psychological, physical, and spiritual. There is no right or wrong when discussing the act of change.

However, many soldiers realize that the change that has occurred within them is not a positive one, and it frightens them to the extent that they question their own ability to make sound judgments. They believe that their moral compass has changed and are afraid it will affect their future life experiences. They believe that the person they were is no longer there and that they have become a different person to the point that they are frightened of this unknown entity.

They must realize that the person at the beginning of the conflict is the same person who returns home. What is changed is that self-judgment becomes more acute and they hold themselves to a higher standard. This is the beginning of a long process of desensitizing themselves to the experiences they have been involved in. Some who have had very high moral standards and who have been in direct conflict with entity combatants and have taken the lives of other humans may have a more difficult time understanding who they really are. They are actually the same people, but because of the situation, they are accurate in feeling that their true selves have been altered to people of a lower moral level. They believe that they were incapable of creating such misery and suffering.

What they must remember is that people who are put into a difficult situation such as a war zone will react to that situation depending on various degrees of involvement. A soldier who has an understanding that he will be involved in the taking of another human's life in participating in acts of violence will be more apt to be able to understand who he is when he returns to civilian life.

It is important to realize that change will occur no matter what situations are experienced in life. Being involved in a war zone will speed up these changes within one's self. Accepting the fact that being involved in a conflict zone is the cause of this change that you feel is the beginning of the process of realizing that life is a learning experience.

Soldiers who are aware of the change that has taken place within them and who accept this change will find it easier to move forward into the next level of life experiences.

This change is an opportunity to look at life with a new perspective and to understand how fragile and short one's time on the Earth plane can be.

For those soldiers who find the change too hard to deal with, it is very important to realize that the experiences they have witnessed were important to the growth of their soul. It may be hard to understand from your perspective, but once it's your time to cross over, you will see how true this really is. Use this opportunity to help others who have gone through life changes that may not be associated with any type of war or conflict but nonetheless have caused suffering to the individual.

Accepting change is the primary goal of self-actualization.

Replace the fear of who you believe you have become with an awareness that your experiences have opened your mind to greater learning experiences that could not have been achieved any other way.

It is important to realize that who you are as a spiritual being has not changed. Only the experiences you have witnessed and live through have changed.

Use the experiences you have witnessed and been involved with as a positive stepping-stone to new experiences. These new experiences can give you the opportunity to bring love and understanding to others around you.

Having experienced certain situations within a war will give you the opportunity to learn to love yourself to a higher degree and to be able to bring relief from suffering to others.

Be a beacon of hope to others who suffer. In doing so, the light you shine will also shine on you and create the peace you so desperately seek.

Chapter 9

I CAN'T COMPREHEND THE THINGS I SAW

We want to give you a brief background on how the mind accesses and interprets certain information. In the case of vision, it has been provided to the human experience for various reasons—one of them being a survival mechanism, and another the ability to acquire information in the shortest period of time. No communication skills are necessary, such as organized language, symbols, or representations. One who uses his visual abilities can distinguish a situation at a moment's notice.

However, when a human is put into a situation in which the information that is being collected is visual, sometimes this information can be transferred so quickly that it may become confused while being accepted. We see this in various situations in which a lot of action on different levels is happening at one time, and one is forced to make a decision very quickly, depending on the visual information that has been received.

In the situation of war, visual input is compounded with the use of other senses, and these, too, can be overwhelming in certain circumstances. One sense, such as vision, may be picking up a particular piece of information, while another sense, such as smell, will be deciphering something entirely different. It is easy in this circumstance for one sense to become overloaded with information, which can cause a disruption in the brain's ability to comprehend the reality of the particular situation. If the sound of explosions are so loud that it creates a physical strain, it may disrupt the brain's problem-solving ability as well.

But what we have found in a combat situation is that, many times, the soldier is overwhelmed with the scene of violence, as it is something he is not used to. Even if he has been in multiple situations of violence, the witnessing of carnage can trigger a negative reaction at any time. The mind may become desensitized to these feelings, but later in time the mind will revisit a particular situation and begin to analyze it for what really happened. You see, the mind has the ability to try to protect the human body—to shut down parts of it in order to save the whole. This is seen in traumatic situations in civilian life as well.

If the mind did not have this ability, a person would not be able to confront certain situations and still have the ability to react as well as continue his life's purpose. Some of the things that are witnessed during times of war and conflict can be of such strain to one's sensibilities that they will cause nightmares and the reliving of certain events. Humans as a whole are not used to witnessing the destruction of others nor being involved in this destruction.

The mind will take time to try to dissect and analyze all the information it has acquired from the bodily senses. When an individual is under extreme trauma for a long period of time, the mind has a way of categorizing and filing away certain events to be analyzed later on. At times the mind is overwhelmed and cannot file away any more events. At that time, the soldier's system begins to shut down. Each individual has different thresholds of when this condition will occur.

Soldiers may feel guilty that they cannot "handle" certain situations as well as their fellow comrades. There are many reasons why individuals have different levels of breaking points. Some depend on how the brain interprets certain information.

Trauma is a complex series of actions that overload the human brain and can remain with an individual for a lifetime. Downloading traumatic information can put undue stress on the human body. As the individual tries to analyze this information and make decisions, the analyzing process becomes more complex, and a shift in reality may occur. Soldiers who were used to relying on a strict decision-making method soon realize that this method is no longer reliable, and this in itself brings doubt and fear. The reality of the situation one has witnessed can overlap with other realities that an individual may be involved in at a later time. Even though two separate situations may have occurred, the mind will try to find similarities between the two, and this can cause distress. It's like a computer filing system; when downloading information and trying to access it later, the information can become corrupt. It may not be the computer itself—it just may be that the system is overloaded.

It's important for soldiers to realize this—that it is not necessarily them, but that the system has been overloaded at some point in time. It could be separate events at different times that may cause the system to go haywire. When this happens, we witness the symptoms of posttraumatic stress syndrome. We also see this in everyday civilian life. When people's information-processing abilities are compromised through stress, emotional turmoil, and other influences, they will show similar symptoms to those of a soldier in a war situation.

Witnessing carnage on a day-to-day basis can desensitize the analyzing process that the mind deals with on a daily basis. When spending some downtime, a soldier may not understand why he is not reacting in a certain way after viewing such violence. This is the soldier performing self-judgment on himself. This is an example of viewing a problem from a shortsighted perspective. When a soldier tries to analyze his environment, his personal feelings, the situations he's been involved in, and his decision making, it is not unusual for him to come to different conclusions. He may come to one conclusion, then doubt it, and the process of self-judgment begins again.

The healing aspect of the situation must start with the realization that the individual soldier should not engage in self-judgment. This self-judgment can bring on other associated issues that can compound the original uneasiness. Questions of guilt, questions of one's ability to be able to handle certain situations, and questions of one's ability to be a kind and loving human are all asked over and over with no sound answer being possible to achieve.

The soldier must step back from the situation that he has been reliving and understand that the stresses he was under while in that situation caused a disruption in the analysis of the information and the sights that were seen. An example of this is what you would call "Monday morning quarterbacking." If we all had the ability to sit back and analyze all our actions and interactions before we did them, we would have the ability to go through life knowing exactly how things play out and with as little pain and suffering as possible. However, no learning experience would take place, as your soul's purpose to learn and grow would stagnate, and your brief period on the Earth plane would have been wasted.

Once one realizes how the process of analysis and the mind works, one can start to understand why certain feelings and emotions continue to bring trauma to oneself. Is important to realize that the downloading of the information one has experienced and witnessed can take time and does not have to be judged at all. And even though we all like to put all our life's experiences into neat little boxes and file them under happy memories, sad events, and even tragedies, this cannot always be done when it comes to one's experiences in war. Realizing this will help in beginning the process of healing.

Just because someone thinks that he's on the road to recovery, this might not always be the case. There'll be setbacks on the road to recovery, and some individuals will see these as failures.

Any setback in a recovery is NOT a failure.
Take conscious action for how you feel.
Remember, some days will be more difficult than others. This is okay.
Ask for help at the first sign of a setback.
It's a process; it takes time, sooner for some, later for others. But at least be on the journey.
Don't look back; otherwise you will trip and stumble into your future.
The things that you have witnessed and experienced are what they are. There doesn't have to be an explanation.

For those who cannot let the trauma go, accept it, and even take it with you, but put it somewhere where you're not going to be tripping over it all the time.

Don't judge yourself. You're not qualified.

"I was a sergeant in the Marine Corps, and I was involved in many brutal battles. I witnessed atrocities that grown men would weep over in just telling the stories. We witnessed the destruction of human beings to the extent that they were like ants to us. We did not take joy in the taking of others' lives but did respond with happiness that we had survived a particular battle. Some of the guys in my unit went crazy. They would break out laughing and continue to do it for hours upon hours. They would be covered in blood and sitting there and laughing at no one in particular.

"It was not out of the ordinary to see some men huddled together and praying. This was their outlet to deal with what they had witnessed during a battle. Some drank, played cards, or slept. Everyone had their own way of dealing with the miserable situation.

"It was tough—one morning you'd be talking to a few of your friends, and by later in the day they would be dead, torn to shreds. It's brutal on the mind, and the next day it could be you. And this can go on for days and weeks and, for some guys, even months. No wonder some of them went crazy. You can't blame them, and you shouldn't blame yourself. Unfortunately that's part of the deal of war.

"I'm not telling you to just forget what happened because, as we both know, that's not going to happen. But remember it in the situation where you were. I was in the mountains dropping bombs on people. When I came home and heard an explosion, I'd jump to the ceiling. Then I realized I wasn't in those mountains anymore—I was home. Now it did take some time to get used to visiting any mountains here at home, but that's another story.

"What I am trying to say is to put it in perspective. If you were lucky enough to make it home, take advantage of that situation. Don't keep going back up to those mountains, or keep going back into that jungle, or walking down that road where you witnessed all that crap. Leave it where it happened—in the past."

Chapter 10
SOME PEOPLE THINK I'M A HERO SOMETIMES I THINK I'M JUST CRAZY

How people judge one another and how they judge themselves are at times totally different. When we look in the mirror and think of the situations we have been involved in, especially situations in which violence has occurred, we can second-guess ourselves as to who we really are. Others who have a different perspective can put us on a pedestal, not realizing that their interpretation of us is totally different from our own interpretation of who we believe we are.

Many times when soldiers return home, certain segments of society will greet them as heroes. This may be associated with different acts and different interpretations. Some may welcome home soldiers who have done battle and completed their missions in a heroic way. Others may welcome soldiers home as heroes just for the fact that they put their lives on the line for their fellow citizens. Each of these may be correct, depending on the circumstances of the era and the conflict in which the soldiers served.

Many times the conflict that a soldier has served in has been controversial. When this has happened, the greeting back home can be more complex for both the soldier and the community welcoming him home. If some feel that the conflict was unjustified, they might take out their frustrations on a returning soldier, even though deep down their frustration and anger are toward their leaders and government. They can use this opportunity to display their opinion to the local face of the controversial conflict, which is the individual soldier.

Many people do, however, feel the compassion and self-sacrifice that the soldier has made in their name. Some may show this appreciation more openly, while others may do it in private. The respect that some feel toward returning soldiers is on an equal level with heroes. People, especially fellow veterans and families who have been through conflict before, have a higher respect and understanding of what the soldier has been through. This is why the soldier has reached the level of a hero in their minds.

A new soldier returning does not have the perspective of being a previous veteran or part of an older military family that might have gone through a similar situation years before. This individual soldier may also still be in conflict about the actions he took while in the war zone. He may not be able to rationalize the threshold of hero with the actions he has taken. Some soldiers may feel quite the opposite—not heroes, but murderers and inflictors of pain and suffering. Some of the actions they took may have been against civilians, which will conflict with their definition of how a hero should act.

This internal conflict can cause undue mental issues for a returning soldier. He may believe he's going crazy or that he's living in a surreal situation, as some people treat him as royalty, and at times he himself feels as if he should treat himself as a person with a low moral code.

The more overt these welcoming actions are, the more enduring the moral conflict may be. If the soldier is highlighted for his heroic actions and does not feel as if he deserved them, his internal conflict can be very deep and long lasting. However, if the soldier believes that the actions he has taken have helped fellow soldiers, shown some level of compassion toward others, or at least held up his obligation to the military, the transition and acceptance of the heroic stature will be a symbol of honor.

In the past, soldiers were more confined and limited in their exposure to the civilian world. The outside judgments that they endured often came from fellow soldiers. To the soldiers, it was more realistic to hear the word *hero* from fellow soldiers than from civilians. However, many times the word *hero* would not be used by a fellow soldier, for he could see that the actions he took were obligations and responsibilities, for which no praise was needed or wanted.

Some soldiers have the attitude that they behaved according to the responsibility that was given to them by the military—that they carried out missions and acts of war in accordance with the rules, regulations, and expectations of their leaders. They are confused by the term *hero* for they see themselves as performing duties for which they have been trained.

Civilians look at the situation of a war conflict and the individuals involved in it and realize that in order to survive it, one must reach the level of heroic status. Civilians may play out these conflicts in their minds hundreds or even thousands of miles away. Their concept of war is slightly askew from that of the soldiers who took part in the active conflict. Civilians have their own doubts and fears concerning conflict, and this is sometimes the cause of their reaction when a soldier returns home and they are inclined to honor him as a hero. In their mind, only a hero could participate in such a serious and violent environment as war.

This is where acclimation of a returning soldier within the community is very important—this transition from a conflict zone and being part of the military brotherhood to returning to the civilian world. At times the soldier may have difficulty understanding how the world has been going on around him and is not more involved in the war conflict that he has just returned from.

In some conflicts, such as world wars, the civilian population has been more involved in the day-to-day issues of conflict than at other times. Even certain areas that have been occupied by outside forces could be seen as returning to normalcy during the conflict. It is common for people to try to return to what they think of as normal, everyday activities in order to reduce the mental stress that surrounds a war.

In eras gone by, soldiers may have served away from their home and family for years. The information they received from their homeland was sparse and limited. Many times situations at home will have changed drastically due to the outcome of the conflict. In cases like this where welcome was not received, soldiers acclimated back into the civilian world with the acceptance that their part in the conflict was over. In these cases, drastic changes had occurred, and the surrealism that modern-day soldiers find themselves in was limited.

The modern soldier can, at times, experience more stress by having access to immediate information concerning his family, homeland, and even the military outcome of various conflicts than by not being in contact at all. This is because the stress can be focused on one area and not on many different fronts.

By being involved in the conflict, you have shown courage.

Taking on this learning lesson is the sign of a hero to us.

Realizing and accepting that you have participated under extreme conditions is important.

Realize that somewhere, at some time, you have supported and helped another, and therefore you are hero to that person. When it comes to hero status, do not self-judge. That term is in the eye of beholder.

Chapter 11
CIVILIANS IN CONFLICT ZONES

Civilians are the group of people who have not engaged in a particular conflict. These are people whom some might label as outsiders, the general population, or people not involved in the conflict. They can include civilians in the middle of a battlefield, civilians surrounding the geographical area of the fight, or civilians who are left at a distant home.

Civilians in a war zone are looked at differently from civilians out of harm's way. People who are in contact with the conflict are at times as oversensitized as the soldier who was actually doing battle. They may appear to be going about their daily lives, but the stress and pressure they are under can be as extreme or more extreme than the stresses that a soldier may witness. For this is their area of living, this is their home, these are their streets, this is their country, and when war breaks out or regional conflict occurs near their home, it brings additional burdens and suffering that civilians from other parts of the world cannot understand or appreciate.

Some of these people have physically been on the battle area around them. Some have interacted with soldiers from either side, and sometimes these interactions have been quite negative. While the civilians try to live active lives, they are also struggling to survive. Many times they have family members who are drawn into this conflict without choice. The civilians have a different concept of war and conflict than soldiers or civilians who are many miles away, living safely in their own districts.

How these civilians deal with war might be totally different than how a soldier might deal with the conflict after he returns home. For civilians in the area of conflict have no recourse as to the outcome of the conflict but rather are bystanders in the middle of a shooting range. Some wish to interact in the conflict, and some do, while others sit back and watch the chaos around them and try to understand how they will survive and keep their families from suffering the carnage that is happening around them.

Many times the civilians adopt survival behaviors that are critical to their existence. These may include engaging in traditional ceremonies, keeping a routine, or allowing the conflict around them to happen while going about their daily lives. Realizing that they cannot control the situation helps them deal with the conflict. They sometimes ask questions of soldiers on both sides, trying to understand what part they play in the situation. They seek to know what is happening and when it will end. Others embrace the change that the conflict will surely bring, even if it is simply the uprising that will take place after the conflict ends. This positive emotion carries them through the disparagement of war.

They see the possibilities in the future, and they see the hope that their children will have in the positive change in their lifestyle. These positive attitudes give them strength to live on a daily basis inside a conflict zone. Others will cower within themselves, as this is the only way they can deal with the outcome of a particular conflict. They have been so overstressed and burdened by being so close to the conflict that their physical senses and thinking abilities have been changed to the point that they are not functioning at a normal level. They cannot deal with the present situation and therefore look inside themselves for peace and stability. They do not care about the outcome of the situation—their only concern is the ability to survive, both mentally and physically. These civilians have a much harder time dealing with this type of conflict than those who are seeking a change and looking forward to the hope of possibilities after the conflict is completed.

Just as soldiers await the return to their homeland, civilians in a conflict zone can't wait to return to the normalcy of everyday living without the bloodshed and screams of neighbors and loved ones that they have witnessed.

Many people may think they can sympathize with the civilian population inside a war zone, but it is difficult if one has not live through it. It is reassuring when civilians speak up and speak out about what has happened to them in order to enlighten the outside world on how conflict and war create not only military casualties but also civilian casualties. This does not even count civilian casualties that are killed as a byproduct of the war itself. These people live in constant danger hour by hour, day by day, not realizing when their time on this plane may be extinguished.

We sympathize with the civilians, as we can feel the anguish from our side, and we can understand the pain and suffering they are going through on a daily basis. Others may write about them in general terms, but we can feel their thoughts and pain on an individual basis, and from here we are able to enlighten others as to the seriousness of this problem.

Civilians coming to grips with being part of a war conflict has changed over time. In eras past, many times these people would be assimilated into the conqueror's way of life and culture. In modern times, many of these civilians continue to practice their own faiths and cultures no matter who is victorious in the battle.

These are just a few insights on how civilians inside combat zones are affected by the conflict. We will talk more about civilians far away from the conflict and how they deal with the situation in another section.

Chapter 12

CIVILIANS AWAY FROM CONFLICT ZONES

Today we will be dealing with civilians who have been left at home. Many of these civilians will be relatives and people you are in relationships with, while others will be the general population of the area you live in or are associated with.

Civilians at home, away from a conflict zone, have a responsibility to those members of the military who are serving in a war zone. Many times we see populations that are disinterested in what their fellow citizens are participating in. At the beginning of a major conflict, the majority of the population might be in total support of the war, but as this war continues on, the strength of that support will wane.

In the past, many nations fought each other on and off for hundreds of years. As new leaders took over positions of authority and wished to expand their power of influence, new conflicts would erupt, and the pattern of a revolving war would continue.

As tactics and weapons increased in their complexity, which we began to see in modern warfare, the actual time of conflicts began to shrink. More missions and actions can be completed in a shorter period of time with the advancement of technology. Even in large conflicts that involve many nations and tens of millions of people, the conflict itself is considerably shorter than conflicts thousands of years ago.

The longer a conflict continues, the more likely that the general population will become acclimated to a nation at war. Everyday living will return to normal, even though fellow citizens are away and facing danger every day. The psyche of the population can only handle a certain length of time of acute awareness. When a population is not directly involved in a conflict, it is easier to go about one's life, dreams, and goals than if one is living in a war zone.

However, to people whose family and friends are directly involved in the conflict, the length of the engagement will not decrease their awareness of and concern about the outcome of the war. They may be located in a safe home environment a vast distance from the battlefield, but they are constantly on guard for information that may affect a loved one or colleague. Their neighbor may be more concerned about civilian life and work, while they are at home worrying about a loved one.

In some past conflicts, the civilian population would only continue to remember the conflict when it personally affected them. We have seen this when armies have taken the majority of food that would otherwise have been distributed throughout the country and used it for the active troops in a distant land. This is an example of how a civilian population that may have the conflict in the back of their mind will now be affected to the point at which it will be important once again.

Many civilians in a safe home environment have a secondary connection to a military conflict. They may work in factories, create military hardware, or have other duties that are related to the event of war. Some of these civilians are reminded on a daily basis of the continuation of the conflict. Not only are some of their jobs based on this conflict, but also the ramifications of their duties can affect their own psyches.

A civilian supporting the troops by sending food and items of enjoyment will feel a bond with the soldiers away at the battlefield. An expression such as "keeping the home fires burning" is important to many civilians who have a connection to the war, even if it's thousands of miles away. They want to relate to the active soldier that they are thinking of him and have not forgotten the connection that was forged when the soldier was home in a safe environment.

People do have a tendency to forget the life of the soldier, especially when a conflict drags on for many years. The populace is not always informed in the proper way of the continuing conflict that causes the death and injury of its citizens. This is the responsibility of leaders in the civilian areas.

Many times civilians in conflict zones will be assaulted with visions and smells of the carnage of war. The modern civilian family living in a safe location will have access to some of these experiences through modern technology, but the experiences will be different. Psychological distress can happen both for the civilian in a war zone and the civilian a safe distance away.

Each has its own characteristics while sharing some common themes. Someone home in a safe environment may feel as if they have no control of the situation, and the stress, anxiety, and worry can manifest to the point of bringing about physical and mental illness. A civilian in the conflict zone will have stress and anxiety from living day-to-day in this environment but may feel that they have more control over their life and therefore does not experience that particular type of stress.

However, it is very important for civilians at home, in a safe location, to be vigilant regarding the continuing active situation within a conflict zone. For when a population begins to disregard the information and knowledge of the reality of the situation occurring to their citizens during battle, an injustice can occur. The reasons for going to war can be skewed, manipulated, and changed without the civilian's knowledge or acceptance.

Just because you don't hear the bombs does not mean they have stopped being dropped.

INSPIRATIONAL MESSAGE I

Your concerns, hopes, and questions are always heard by us. We have attempted to answer some of your questions in this book, and we will continue to work with each one of you in trying to bring peace and healing. Do not feel as though you are alone. You are always connected to us, you are always connected to spirit, you are always connected to yourself, for you are spirit.

Chapter 13
WE DON'T ALL FEEL THIS WAY, BUT SOME OF US DO

Joe, it is our understanding that returning veterans will have different issues. What we mean by this is that different experiences will resonate at different levels, depending on the person who was involved. One soldier might have a different experience in a conflict than another soldier, and therefore his reactions to his involvement in that conflict will differ from those of other soldiers. It's not uncommon for some soldiers who have not seen combat to have similar anxiety to those who have been in conflict, for the urge to be part of the group is so strong that they can feel the association with the combat veteran. People think that a soldier who has not witnessed the atrocities of war should not have to deal with trauma after returning home. Many of these soldiers will suffer in silence for fear of being ridiculed since their experiences do not match the severity of other soldiers' experiences.

How one soldier will acclimate to the civilian world will differ from a soldier who might make the military his career. The variation revolves around how environment plays an important role in how he acclimates to his new life. Some soldiers who have experienced violent acts of war may not have symptoms and changes as severe as those of others who fought by their side. Some may have similar symptoms, and others may have more acute, disabling effects.

There are different levels of acceptance of what soldiers have experienced. We know that crossover effects happen to soldiers who may not have had the same experiences in a particular conflict but who share the same trauma. We also know that soldiers from different wars and conflicts throughout history may share the same symptoms with other soldiers.

It's important for the veteran to understand that what he feels is real—it is real to his own experience and his own feelings. While some may want to categorize certain experiences as happening to certain soldiers, the most important thing is that the soldier himself realize that his individual experience is true. Knowing this will help when it comes to the healing process that we hope this book will initiate.

Do not ever feel as though you're alone. Many soldiers feel isolated because they don't fit into a particular category of symptoms and experiences that others think they should fit into. You're an individual, a spirit, and it is you who has to deal with the events that you have experienced.

So when working on the idea of why some people feel the way they do and others don't, take this into consideration, both for yourself and for others. With this information, you can see where certain people are coming from and understand some of their problems that perhaps you could not see due to your perspective.

Support yourself and one another—this is the key to this statement.

Understand that it is okay to feel the way you do.

No one has the authority to tell you how you should or should not feel.

You should not judge others with your perspective on how they should feel.

Bring comfort to those in need, even if you do not understand their difficulties.

Why do some feel this way and others don't? Because each one of you is an individual—an individual spirit.

Chapter 14

AM I LESS OF A SOLDIER IF I DID NOT SEE HAND-TO-HAND COMBAT?

There are different degrees of involvement in war. Some can be direct, such as hand-to-hand combat, while others can be in a support role. Oftentimes we hear soldiers after they have returned home think about their involvement in the conflict and their role in the conflict. Oftentimes they will interact with other returning soldiers as well as veterans from past conflicts and talk about some of their experiences.

Some might begin to feel guilty that their involvement was not more personal or in depth. Some soldiers may relate their horrific experiences and how they conquered those experiences to make it home. Others will listen to those experiences and try to relate to them but can only listen, as they have not had that type of experience themselves.

Some soldiers in supporting roles may have not been to the front lines, and some may not have even been in a conflict zone. They may have been stationed in a geographical area that was far away from the fighting and violence. Their role might have been in communications, supply, or other assets that are needed to carry out various missions during the time of conflict.

Some will begin to self-judge their involvement in the war as not equal to those with experience physically engaging with the enemy. They might even consider themselves less of a veteran or soldier than their counterparts who were on the front lines. This is another example of self-judgment. What these soldiers do not realize is the importance of their role in the overall conflict.

It is important to remember that one's role in war cannot be easily chosen by the individual soldier. There are chains of command that will delegate certain activities to certain individuals and groups. An example of this is an infantry unit, which will have a higher percentage of engagement with the enemy than a person assigned to a radar installation group who may be observing the enemy from a secured location.

Are both of these groups needed in a war situation? The simple answer is yes. Throughout time, all conflict has had different groups involved in the management of the war. The technology and tactics may have changed, but many military establishments are separated into different specialties, some being picked to engage the enemy one-on-one.

The experiences that an individual soldier has will be directly connected to the level of involvement he has been entrusted to carry out. Soldiers in an environment in which their senses have been overloaded with intense information will have a higher chance of medical disturbance than soldiers who have been involved in the conflict from a distant location.

When a soldier becomes involved in war, he begins to share a bond with his fellow soldiers. They might not be directly involved in the fighting, but they still share that important bond. That bond is actually shared not only through military personnel but also civilians in the area and civilians related to the soldiers involved in the fighting. The bond might even be between nation states, cultures, and other groups that have a common attachment to the situation.

Are you less of a soldier or veteran for not being directly involved in the fighting? No, once you become involved in the conflict, you become a veteran of that situation, for one individual group cannot wage war without the support and backup of other groups.

Some soldiers who, in their line of duty, have made decisions and who have added to the information and knowledge needed to complete a mission have thoughts about this duty leading to loss of life. An example of this may be a reconnaissance team. They may not have been directly involved in the interaction with the enemy, but their involvement would have cause the loss of life. Throughout the ages, certain groups in the military have used different techniques to engage the enemy without themselves being in any direct danger.

Some soldiers may believe that their personal experiences during the time of war are more important than those of some of their fellow soldiers. They may believe that their influence should be rated at a higher degree than others. Some believe that their actions are far superior to those soldiers stationed far away from enemy lines. These soldiers may have a higher opinion of themselves for various reasons. Civilians sometimes judge themselves superior to other civilians, and this also happens within the confines of the military.

One's involvement in a war will eventually come down to each individual's understanding of his interactions during that time. Each must realize what part he played in the conflict. He alone must adjust back to the civilian world when it is time to end his military commitment.

Some of the soldiers will have to deal with not only answering and being judged by civilians but also having to answer and be judged by their fellow veterans. This judgment can be harsh, and at times it may cause a soldier to exaggerate his involvement in a conflict.

It is important to realize that each soldier will have to decide how he wants to handle his experiences. Talking to fellow soldiers in similar situations can help in understanding where they may have fit in the bigger picture of war.

Being honest with oneself and looking at the facts are also important in realizing one's involvement in the conflict. Realizing that the commanding staff may have chosen where to place you during the conflict, with no control of that decision on your part, should always be remembered.

The realization that the soldier has performed to the best of his ability is important in determining how that soldier will feel about himself. Even if a soldier believes he could have acted and performed at a higher level, he might not realize that under certain conditions he was not allowed to. This is where the perspective of the individual soldier is not always as keen as we see it on the other side. We can see how different parts of the whole work together when the individuals don't always know the whole story.

Once a soldier, always a soldier.
One cannot engage in war by themselves.

All soldiers start with basic training; some training may be different in different military groups, but all begin with the basics.

Someone in a tank cannot control that vehicle if it has no fuel. Some other soldier has had to provide the fuel and parts for the vehicle to be used.

A soldier cannot engage the enemy one-on-one if prior knowledge has not been given to him of the location of the enemy. This location may not be pinpointed; it may be a general area, but work and time have been put in by others to support those who meet the enemy one-on-one.

The weapons you use in war are sometimes created by civilians, perhaps in a distant land. Some of these civilians contemplate how the weapons they are manufacturing will be used and who will be killed by them as a result of the civilians' actions. Some civilians will not be able to sleep at night, knowing that the gun they have just produced will enable someone to kill and maim other humans. To others, it may just be a job, but many times this problem goes unnoticed.

Many people play a part when engaging in conflict or war. You're not alone, and you will always be connected to those who have participated at some level in the war effort.

Chapter 15

RELATIONSHIPS AND HOW THEY'RE AFFECTED

We talk about relationships and how it's important to understand that dealing with grief and suffering can affect more than just the individual. While one individual may rationalize and deal with a situation in one manner, another individual may deal with it in a totally different way.

We see this especially in dealing with the subject of war and conflict. Many times individuals in relationships are separated when one is sent to a war zone while another remains in a safe environment. The emotional needs of the individuals are different at these times. Although the connection between the two is geographically distant, their spiritual connection is still as close as when they were together physically. Outside stimuli, such as being directly involved in a conflict or not knowing if your loved one is in harm's way, can put harsh pressure on the relationship on all levels.

From the soldier's perspective, he seeks the safety of his home, family, and friends in his mind as chaos erupts around him. From the perspective of a loved one in the security of a distant home they deals with emotions related to the unknown. They go through phases of guilt, anger, and frustration in not being able to support their partner or relative in the way that they feel they should.

Parents of soldiers have certain emotions that may differ from those of a partner or spouse. Children who are old enough to understand the circumstances will also experience difficulties in adjusting to the situation. The soldier will have a circle of friends with whom he will serve and be in extreme conditions, and this will bring about a closeness among this particular group. Being exposed to the stresses of war will bring together a group of soldiers who will trust and rely upon each other as if they were of the same blood and family. This is the environment they are in, and it is a natural relationship that is built upon common experiences. The soldiers will also have emotional difficulties when one of their family members from this group is harmed or killed.

So what we see is various people in various relationships sharing similar and specific dealings with someone who is in a conflict area. Many will share the same emotional ups and downs, such as missing their loved ones to concern for safety, guilt, and fear of the unknown. Some experiences will be slightly different, such as that of a parent whose child is in the military and the soldier who has left children at home for a particular period of time.

These individuals face many different challenges on a daily basis. Some turn to their faith, others to the community for support, and some to their friends for laughter and understanding. These types of relationships under the stress of war have been going on since the beginning of time. As war and conflict bring out specific adjustments that must be made in order for these relationships to be healthy and stay focused on, what is most important is the love that is shared between the individuals.

At times, people feel overwhelmed with the stresses that these relationships can cause and seek out unhealthy releases in order to deal with their fears and uncertainties. These unhealthy releases can include drugs and alcohol abuse as well as emotional outbursts that can cause various types of strain on the relationships. Some individuals will become isolated, while others will become highly involved in the war effort. Some will seek answers from outsiders while trying to understand how their relationship will be able to not only last but to thrive as they once had.

There are various ways of dealing with relationships inside a war zone. People have realized the importance of continuing the relationships they have with the civilian world. Leaders and military personnel realize that soldiers are more able and healthy if they can interact with civilian relations on a periodic basis. This, they believe, lifts a burden of stress off the minds of soldiers. The leaders believe that by relieving soldiers of stress, they will be better able to focus on the particular mission and what needs to be accomplished on the military field.

This strategy also helps those at home to continue a relationship with their loved ones in the war zone. With today's technology, being able to see a spouse or parent through various methods brings a measure of relief to the burden of not having that person actually home with them. To be able to talk to the soldier and see him in a faraway land at a moment's notice is very reassuring to both individuals.

There will always be problems when people involved in relationships are separated for a significant period of time. When you add in the uncertainty and safety of an individual, it compounds the emotional distress that is felt by both parties. This is something that is unique to war. Many individuals have become stronger due to the absence and the learning experience they are involved in, while some relationships have crumbled under the stresses put upon them by various incidents that have arisen during the time of departure.

It is helpful for an individual to try to put the relationship in perspective within the confines of war. Certain aspects of the relationship will change, and this needs to be noted so as not to add to the stresses of the separation. One partner is not going to be home to help with household chores or run errands, and the other has not chosen to put their life in danger over the love of their spouse. These are aspects of a relationship that can become clouded and enshrouded in guilt. If these types of examples are understood, the relationship can more easily move forward to a higher level that is needed in this type of circumstance.

People sometimes put too great a burden on themselves, not knowing how their relationship will change once they are reunited with a loved one. This can put a high level of stress on the relationship. It is better if the individuals take it one day at a time and live the experience together as opposed to trying to understand the concept of separation.

The difficulties brought about through war affect individuals on different levels. When individuals understand what others are trying to deal with, it helps in the relationship and can diffuse potential problems.

Try to understand that things will be different, and that's okay.

Some relationships will blossom, and some will deteriorate, but there is always hope.

Understanding what someone has been through is not as important as supporting that person as an individual.

If each of you backs up the other, success is assured.

You will change. Accept that as the first step.

There are new learning opportunities when stress is placed on a relationship.

Help is available—seek it.

Don't judge a broken relationship. It may be meant as a learning experience.

Joe, it is difficult when some spouses return home to civilian life. They have changed as individuals, and so have the loved ones who have been left at home. Many times people focus on the fact that the soldier has been through a transitional period on a physical and emotional level, but they forget about the fact that the civilians who have been at home have also been through a transitional period on an emotional and psychological level. These changes might not be as evident as those of the returning soldiers, but they are still real and important and need to be considered. They need to be considered by the community and especially by the returning soldier. As civilians are aware of trying to help a returning combat soldier back into civilian life, everyone must realize that both parties in the relationship need help, both together and separately.

This is not a time for judgment, guilt, or blame. The growth in healing of a relationship that has been put under extreme stress through the departure of a loved one into a war zone and then his return home can be successful if all parties realize that they must work with each other as well as on themselves alone.

Chapter 16

BEING BRAVE DOESN'T MEAN NOT HAVING TO ASK FOR HELP

Being brave is not an act in itself. Bravery can be classified in different ways. Some people consider bravery the act of protecting others who are not strong enough to take care of themselves. Some people think bravery is putting others' lives ahead of your own. Others believe bravery is taking a stand for something they believe in, even though by taking this stand, they will be attacked and discriminated against.

Bravery comes in all sizes and shapes. Some people who show bravery are the smallest of children, and others are well-trained, physically massive soldiers. What we want to talk about today is how people of all occupations and cultures have the ability to show bravery in their everyday lives.

Some people have difficulty in dealing in their daily lives and seek help from others in order to improve their life's condition. When people seek out the help of others for personal reasons in order to better themselves, this is a great sign of courage and bravery. Some might think of this as a weakness in not being able to deal with a certain situation by themselves. But actually, by asking others for help, it shows strength that you have concern for yourself. It is easier to suffer silently and not to seek out the help of others than it is to ask for help in the first place.

We can help many of you with the suffering that you're currently enduring—all you need to do is ask. If you do not ask, we cannot intercede. All it takes is a simple prayer or a simple sentence. Many of you have been through many physical and emotional experiences that you have survived and think that you can handle the orientation back into civilian life as you handled the circumstances during your experiences in the conflict. People are asked sometimes why they seek help while others do not need it. The remaining reason for this is that sometimes the people who are helping you are learning their own lessons and thus you are helping them achieve purposes on a higher level.

When you ask for help, it is not always for yourself; the others around you who assist you are themselves accessing higher levels of learning. There is a reason why they are there to help others who have experienced things that you have. They are there to learn and guide you and others. So by not stepping up and accessing this help, you're actually taking away learning experiences from those people who help counsel, guide, and relieve the suffering of others.

Weakness is never associated with asking for help. Take this from our side—we know from experience. Being alone in suffering when there is assistance available is a tragedy. If a fellow soldier needed assistance on the battlefield, would you help him? If a fellow soldier needed assistance in civilian life, would you help him? Then why wouldn't you give assistance to the counselors, guides, and fellow veterans who try to help you in reorganizing your life? Asking for assistance is part of the process; it should not even be related to the concept of bravery. You have already shown your bravery when you were born. You might not have realized it until you began to experience extreme conditions. But every day of human existence is a form of bravery for your soul. Some build on that experience and lead others and bring compassion and loving to those around them. These are strong individuals who have chosen to take the path that they see is the right way in order to help others. Helping others, relieving suffering, and thinking of others' lives ahead of one's own are all bravery.

Don't for one second give any credence or listen to anyone who considers asking for help to be a weakness. That is an excuse for their inability to reach out and assist others with their problems. People who consider this a weakness are disassociating themselves from the reality of the interaction between individuals on a physical as well as spiritual level. In order for you to grow as a person, spiritually and physically, you must follow your inner compass. Do not let others adjust this compass for you. Follow your heart—this is bravery. Take the risk that you are afraid of by seeking help—this is bravery.

Try different forms of assistance. If one method does not work, it does not mean another method will also not work. As a veteran, you've been told many times to do things over and over until you get them right. Use the same training to get help for yourself. Try things over and over until you get them right.

We will talk about the different avenues for seeking help in another part of this book. But you must first realize that the act of asking for help, and the opportunity to assist you, is one of the highest forms of bravery. You are all born with this ability, and you can tap into it at any time. It is a tool that you have brought to this physical plane. You must practice using this tool; it is there to assist you so you can continue on your path of learning.

Use your newfound bravery to help others complete their learning process and to bring peace and relief from suffering to your fellow veterans who are in need at this time.

And do not forget that the civilians in your life—your family, love ones, and coworkers—have also shown a form of bravery as they seek answers to some of the most difficult questions concerning war and conflict. They also need to reach out and ask for assistance when it is necessary and not feel as if it's a sign of weakness. Just because they did not experience the same events that a soldier in battle has experienced does not mean that they don't have underlying suffering and pain.

You as a veteran also have the responsibility to help others around you when you see them suffering because not only are you a brother to your fellow veterans but you are also part of the human race. You also have a responsibility to others who seek out your help and others who are too afraid or too hurt to ask for assistance. Seek out those fellow souls and assist them in coming to terms with who they are in order for them to continue on their learning paths.

For your assistance in helping yourself and helping others will bring you to a higher level of existence, which you will not realize until you cross to our side. We have seen it and experienced it, and we are giving you insight into the process and giving you the ability to work with the tools you already have in order to relieve the suffering and pain that exist for so many.

We leave you with this phrase to ponder: If all of you would only give assistance to those who have helped you in the past, you would not only be on an island alone, but you would be on a ship that was sinking. For you ought to give assistance to each other even if you have never met them before. By assisting and asking for assistance, you interact at the highest personal levels, and this is where miraculous events can occur. Your mind will open up, your heart will realize the difference that you made in this world, and this will set you forward on your path of learning and understanding.

Chapter 17

WILL GOD JUDGE ME FOR KILLING OTHERS?

Joe, we realize this is the type of question that is often asked by both civilian and military personnel. The question of whether one individual will be held accountable for taking the life of another human being is a question we constantly get from people who have the ability to show compassion and empathy toward others.

When soldiers and other individuals are placed in the arena of war or other conflict, it is part of the circumstances at that time to take part in transforming another human from his physical presence back to his spiritual makeup. This might sound technical for a soldier killing an enemy combatant, but we see it from a different perspective. We see one human being ending the physical existence of another human being.

The circumstances of this action is where the focus should be. By this, we mean that the random killing of another individual for one's own selfish purposes will have to be taken into account once that individual crosses over himself. He will see what actions he has caused and what suffering he has permitted to take place because of his actions.

However, when individuals are involved in a war situation and must, at times, take action to protect themselves or others from dire consequences and these actions involve the taking of another human's life, they will not be asked to justify their actions after passing to our side.

When one enters the realm of the nonphysical world, physical life is looked at from a different perspective.

People have a tendency to judge themselves for the actions they have taken in vastly different situations. Killing another human being in the arena of war is much different from taking another human being's life in the civilian world. There may be similarities for certain individuals, such as a police officer or someone protecting a neighbor or a loved one. The taking of an individual's life inside a conflict zone is judged to be a reaction to the circumstances at the time.

However, there are instances in which soldiers become acclimated to the point of enjoying or getting emotionally high from the taking of a life and inflicting unnecessary suffering on others. These particular individuals will be asked to answer for their actions once they have crossed to the other side. They will be faced with the consequences of having to see the suffering they have inflicted on others. They will have to judge themselves as to the conduct they have initiated.

God—or, as some may perceive, a higher intelligence—will oversee this process, and the individual himself will be held accountable by himself. With a new perspective that he has on the other side, he will be able to look at his human life experiences from a different angle and see and feel the suffering he has caused. For those who accept this responsibility, the learning process will continue, and the ability for their soul's growth will be allowed to move forward.

However, for those who do not wish to take responsibility for their actions or understand the reasons why these actions were taken, their soul's growth will stop. They will not be allowed to continue in their growth until they understand the cause and effect that they created on the Earth plane.

However, most soldiers and other individuals who killed within a violent conflict zone will not have to be categorized at this level. Even if some become numb to the killing that they had experienced and been involved with, these are physical and mental conditions that will be examined once the soldiers have crossed over. They will understand that the circumstances they were under and the pressures and stresses they witnessed caused the reactions that they might think were unnecessary at the time. They will realize the lessons from these events and will move forward in their soul's growth to a high level.

At first, they may seem highly judgmental of themselves for their conduct, not realizing that the stress in the environment in which the action took place was the motivating factor. Many times, individuals believe that by killing someone else, even in a war zone, they have committed a so-called sin against humanity. This is not the case. Many factors have to be weighed in the judgment of taking another's life. In a war or conflict zone, these factors are multiplied and can be difficult to separate.

The healing process can also begin on this plane before one passes by realizing that the actions that one has taken inside a conflict area were brought about because of various circumstances. They may consist of a particular mission plan or a strategy but might also have involved environmental issues, stress, emotional issues, and various other influences at that particular time.

It is important to realize once again not to judge oneself so harshly as to become emotionally paralyzed and not be able to continue your learning lessons here on the Earth plane. You should and can continue with a life of growth and enjoyment, even after witnessing or being involved in such a violent conflict. Many soldiers think that they will never be able to overcome the actions they have taken under duress, and we can say that this is not true. You have an obligation to yourself and your loved ones and family to realize that the judgment you have handed down upon yourself has resulted from holding this singular perspective. Once you have crossed over, your perspective will have changed, and you will be seeing the situation for what it really was. There were reasons for your conduct that you cannot comprehend right now that will be revealed to you. But you still must continue your soul's growth on the Earth plane. It is essential to your growth overall and to the growth of others around you. This is important—you must realize that others who interact with you are also learning, and you are responsible to help not only yourself but also others around you reach their potential.

So, to use the word *judgment*, you must look at it in perspective—how you think about and judge yourself on this plane, at this time—for your reactions in a violent situation will be different from the perspective you will see on the other side when it is your time to cross over. There you will see the realities of your actions and reactions, and will see that there were more circumstances impacting what you participated in than you were able to perceive while on the Earth plane.

Don't be too harsh on yourself. You'll eventually find deeper meaning in your actions.

Judging is the wrong word. It's more like viewing your participation in your life's Earth experiences.

It's not the number of people you've killed—it's how you went about it and the intention behind the killing.

There'll be worse things in life than killing an enemy combatant. Giving up on life's opportunities for learning is one of those things.

"Joe, I accepted what I did and moved on. I had to—there was no other way to survive. It's crazy when you think about it. I mean, you have to rationalize killing other people. If I had to do it over again, hell no, I wouldn't want to do it again. But now I can see the purpose of me having to go through that experience. There is so much more involved than just the act of killing. People don't realize this—they want to put a bull's-eye around the act itself without looking at the bigger picture. We are here to interact with other people, and sometimes those interactions can be violent, but that's the way life is supposed to be.

"I know a lot of guys who didn't make it home, and I eventually saw them over here. They were not pissed that they got killed—they were home. They didn't care who shot them or blew them up; it didn't make any difference at all to them. They just look back at the experiences they had learned from while on Earth.

"It really didn't matter who killed them. So if you didn't matter to them, why does it matter to you? Because you care, which is a good thing, but don't let it hold you back and destroy your life.

"I can't take my life back and change it the way I want to. It's gone. I have to move on to other experiences. So take my advice: Don't think of the guy you took out because he doesn't waste a millisecond thinking about you. If you learn to be more compassionate from your experiences and that's good, that's what it's all about. You see, sometimes real love and caring come out of misery and horrendous circumstances.

"There's this guy named Jimmy who hasn't gotten over some of the crap that he did. He's been messed up his whole life, and this shit has been eating at him every single day. He can still change; he can still accept what he did and realize that the pain and suffering he inflicted are gone. The only pain left is the pain he gives himself each day. I can see it on his face; I can feel it in his body. Joe, you got to let this guy know he's okay.

"I'm going to give some information that no one else knows about this guy so when he reads this, he will know it's about him.

"The dude was a mother fuckin' bad dude—he was truly nuts, suicidal. He loved to kill, he love to butcher people. He didn't care—he would just mow people down. He didn't care how many were out there—he just keep firing with all kinds of shit flying by him. He was a wrecking crew.

"He took out a bunker one time, I swear, with his bare hands. He ran out of ammo, just jumped in the bunker and stabbed the guy. Fuckin' crazy. He spent a lot of time trying to figure out the shit he went through. Joe, he acted like a machine in combat, but back at home he was meek. He didn't do shit, he couldn't take care of himself, and he just brutalized himself. But you couldn't kill that mother fucker, and he is still alive today.

"So Jimmy, this is for you. Listen up, you did what you had to do, but you haven't finished the job. You got to fix your head. It's the last thing you got to do—look in the mirror and say, 'I'm done beating myself up. It's over.'

"This is from your buddy Bradley—we were in basic together. (He says this smiling, saying he is going to blow this guy's mind when he realizes who is talking to him.)

"You've wasted enough time. Give it a break, take a rest, for Christ's sake, and will you smile once in awhile?"

Chapter 18

WHEN IT'S MY TIME TO CROSS OVER, WILL I SEE THE PEOPLE I KILLED?

This particular question you ask is of utmost importance to many people who have been involved in conflict. Soldiers in particular will lament the idea that a casualty they caused will in some way come back and affect their current or future life. Some may think that it might bring about bad karma, while others think they will be punished for eternity. They believe that the actions they have perpetuated on this plane will cause them suffering in the future and in the afterlife.

They must understand that their actions at a particular time and place can affect their future development in a positive or negative way. This is not to say that the killing of another human being will necessarily create a negative ripple in the development of the soul. It is in the concept of war and conflict that many of these ideals take on new perspectives about death.

People have wanted to know since the beginning of time if the taking of someone's life is in itself a negative aspect on one's soul. For our purpose here, we will highlight the effect it has on the soul's learning in the area of war and conflict. The taking of another person's life in the civilian world for no apparent reason other than one's own selfish advantage would be considered a negative ripple in one's own self-development. However, when a life is taken in the realm of war or conflict, this is not always the case.

There are instances in which a soul will be adversely affected by the taking of another's life in war. We see this sometimes when the soldier may act out outside the borders of his duties in order to inflict pain and suffering that are unnecessary. These are cases in which the individual is responsible for his actions, and it will be noted for him when he crosses over and sees the larger perspective of his life. He will have to answer for these indiscriminate acts of inhumanity.

Soldiers who act out under the stresses of war are not held as responsible as those who manipulate the situation for their own benefit. These benefits can be self-serving and just focused on their personal inability to recognize the value of another life.

Some soldiers may believe that their actions are inhumane after they have been involved in a conflict and have inflicted much damage and suffering. This is not the case. They have been put in this situation for various reasons, which we will talk about in other sections of the book. These reasons are learning opportunities on a variety of different levels. However, the soldier who is in the act of performing these duties or acts of violence becomes traumatized by what he has done. He must realize that what he has done has not come from his soul but is a reaction to the situation and environment that he was in. This in itself will bring learning lessons to the individual. But one must not judge oneself for reacting in the proper manner in that situation. Soldiers have been trained to react the way they have—they have a mission to accomplish that can cause harm and casualties. This is part of the process and intricacies of war and conflict.

The individual soldier might get caught up in how he personally can explain to himself his actions without seeing how those actions are part of a bigger plan—part of a mission or strategy within the conflict. If the soldier is performing his duties as he has been trained to do in the realm of the conflict situation, he is given a "special pass," as you may say, when it comes to the development of his soul.

When one passes to our side, he is greeted by many friends, relatives, and loved ones, some he has never met on the Earth plane. He will be reunited with close allies who have spent time with him on our plane but who may not have existed on the human plane. They are there to comfort and welcome the soul back to its original place of existence. When one arrives, one has a larger perspective of one's life on the Earth plane. Part of this perspective is looking over accomplishments, opportunities, and lessons throughout one's life. If someone has been involved in war and conflict, these emotions and events will be looked at from a new perspective.

Soldiers who may be ashamed or afraid of what they will face when they cross over are looking at their lives from the perspective of someone living their life now on the Earth plane. This perceptive will change once they have crossed over. They will realize that some of the actions they took were necessary at the time they happened. Those actions will not weigh on them as they have weighed on them while living on the Earth plane.

Individuals will meet others who have existed on the Earth plane at the same time they existed. They may be coworkers, friends, or fellow soldiers. They may even be individuals considered to be the enemy in a conflict they once fought in. To an individual living on the Earth plane, this type of meeting may sound as if it would be disruptive and uneasy. However, what we have found is that this meeting is very healing, comforting, and intimate when it happens on our side.

Soldiers who come into contact with people they have killed on the Earth plane are shocked to find that their victims are there to support them in their crossing. This may be confusing to those living on the Earth plane now, but when they cross over, they realize that there is a connection between everyone.

The name of this book, *Always Connected,* matches this description perfectly. It is not the *fact* of seeing individuals whom you have caused harm and death to, but it is your *relationship* to them that will be different from what you assume it will be. Many soldiers assume that if they see an individual they have killed or caused harm to, they will experience it as hurtful and harmful. Soldiers do not have to worry about this meeting. There is great support and understanding when the two have the opportunity to meet each other.

A soldier is not forced to meet the so-called victims whom he perceives that he caused harm to. However, it is often a very healing moment that is initiated by the soldier himself. You will learn that the opportunity to meet some of the people whom you caused death and suffering to will be the ones who will bring you the greatest healing.

If the act of killing in a conflict situation brings you great joy on a deeper level, your reunion with the victims will not be as helpful in your healing as if you were going about your job as a trained soldier. This should not be confused with the delight and joy of realizing that you survived the conflict situation nor with the fact that you have attained the level of success that your mission required. These are natural emotions that are part of the concept of war and conflict.

It is when you become enamored of the infliction of pain and suffering that you do the most damage to your soul growth. Many times people of lower soul development may become more aroused in seeing others in pain and suffering. These particular individuals have come to the Earth plane with fewer tools and less growth experience than those around them. These lower forms of entities can cause chaos in the development of others around them. Some of these entities will not move on and grow but will continue to affect those around them in a negative way. These entities that take the form of humans relish in seeing death, destruction, and harm come to others.

If someone is concerned about how he will be judged on the other side, he does not have to worry that his makeup is of a lower level, for he shows compassion on some level to others he has interacted with. Even those who become numb to conflict and war will begin the healing process and growth at some time.

Do not let the thought of seeing others you have come in conflict with when you pass to the other side disrupt your learning opportunities on the Earth plane right now. It's important to realize that they will in fact be part of the healing and growing process once you have crossed over. Realize this and the healing can begin here on the Earth plane and will continue once you've crossed over. It is important to realize that you are always connected, even to those whom you have never met.

Chapter 19

I FEEL THE SUFFERING
THAT I INFLICTED UPON PEOPLE

Joe, the reason the returning soldiers sometimes have this concern is related to how they will judge themselves after inflicting pain and suffering on other human beings. You see, they don't understand the processing mechanism.

Part of the process of growth—soul growth—is to learn firsthand from experiences. On the other hand, people understand the *concepts* of inflicting pain and suffering on other humans. So when the two combine to create learning experiences, there is a residual effect that happens. Soldiers at times will be asked to do things that they cannot imagine—things that will involve inflicting pain, suffering, and emotional distress on others. Some of these experiences can be so traumatic and vivid that the soldiers may describe them as a nightmare or being in hell. (We use this terminology so you will understand the information we are passing over to you. The subject of nightmares and the essence of the location referred to as "hell" are something we will not discussed right now because it is not necessary.)

As people encounter violence in a conflict area and realize that they are the cause and instigators of this violence, it begins to trigger questions within their minds. They begin to ask themselves how they are able to inflict such mayhem on a fellow human being. Even though that other person may be considered the enemy, and they may be responsible for atrocities against civilians or fellow soldiers, there is still a deep-down misunderstanding of how one can inflict such pain and suffering as they have experienced.

Many times this analysis of the situation will take place on the battlefield, but most often it becomes more vivid and confusing as the soldier returns to civilian life. This is where there is a greater contrast between a battlefield situation and a calmer, more secure environment such as being back in their home environment.

When these thoughts occur to a soldier on the battlefield, they are soon replaced with the reality that he himself is still in a position to be killed. Therefore, his attention returns to the reality of the situation in order to avoid harm to himself. When the soldier has return to civilian life, there will be times when these memories will recur, and there will not be any high-priority stimulus to detract from the surfacing of these experiences.

An example of this may be witnessing the killing and maiming of soldiers in a battle and then moving forward into different positions and preparing for a future attack. The soldier's mind is busy with decisions and actions that he has been trained to carry out. When the memory returns to him as a civilian, he may be alone walking down the street and have the ability to make random choices that will not be live-or-die decisions. So he will have more time to concentrate on the actions he took under the extreme conditions of war.

One of the ways the soldier may try to relieve the thought of the suffering he has inflicted on others is to try to inflict that same pain on himself. By reliving the situation, he begins to judge himself and then also begins to set his own punishment. There are many levels of the psyche that are involved in the situation. We do not want to confuse your readers by going into the details of how the mind interacts with itself in deciphering this type of information. At some time in the future, we could begin to explain this process to the masses, but it would have to be set apart from this particular subject matter.

So as the soldier remembers experiences he has witnessed and participated in concerning inflicting pain and suffering on other individuals, he will analyze how he would feel if someone had inflicted that pain on him. This is how he relates to another human being.

Some veterans can analyze this information and come to the conclusion that these events took place under much stress in an area of conflict and the choices were very limited regarding how he could carry out his mission without inflicting the suffering. These veterans realize there is no need to punish themselves in order to relieve the memories. They take their actions for what they were—that they were only related to a certain time, place, and activity. They have a much easier time in acclimating back to society after being part of a violent exchange inside a conflict zone.

Others who cannot understand what has happened to them will begin to mix the memories of the experiences they were involved in with other memories of other experiences. Commingling these experiences can increase the disturbance the soldier brings upon himself. The more the soldier continues to judge and punish himself, the longer this effect will be active in his life.

At some point, it actually becomes a self-perpetuating illness. And as the cycle begins, it becomes more difficult to intervene in and stop the suffering.

The best way to deal with the situation is to talk about it. Explain what has occurred to yourself, a friend, a professional, or God. Talk about it, lay it out. If it has to be dealt with, then you must deal with it. Don't let it hide and fester inside your psyche. This is where it can become more difficult and more intertwined with other emotions and events in your life. But by dealing with it straight out, one situation at a time, there is a higher probability that the suffering can be relieved. Don't bury it deep down, thinking that it will not resurface. You don't necessarily have to come to an understanding of the situation you have been a part of; just accepting the fact that you're aware of it is enough to put it in its place.

Don't act like it didn't happen—it did.

Let it go and move on. Don't deny it—just release your grip on it.

By continuing to hurt yourself in self-judgment, you will bring suffering and pain to the people you love.

You might think it's all about you, but your friends and family feel it, too.

We are not asking you to forget it—just give yourself a break.

Anger is not going to solve anything. It will just increase your burden.

You're not alone. Many of us have experienced the same things and same thoughts and doubts as you. And we know what you're going through. We are here to listen to your anger, frustration, and suffering. We can see how it is not necessary. We see the importance of not judging oneself. It really will affect great opportunities that you will miss in life. So much happiness is wasted on people judging themselves about prior actions that they really didn't have any control over. And if you're in a war zone, you don't have any control. You may think you do, and you may actually make decisions you think you have control over, but you don't. Because those decisions are altered by your environment, your training, and the chemical reactions that are taking part in your brain.

"Joe, my name is Brendan, Army fifth infantry. Listen, I saw a lot on the battlefield, and I did my just part in causing enough pain and suffering to last multiple lifetimes. You see, what happens, Joe, is once you get going and the killing begins, it actually can become routine. For some people, it never will be, but for others, it's just how we coped. If there were fifty guys over that hill who want to cut my head off, I'm not to think about how inflicting pain and suffering on them is going to affect me later on. Shit, I'm going to just blow them away. And the next fifty guys get the same thing. Keep coming and I'll keep wasting them. See, you don't have time on the battlefield to get all sensitive and weepy—you just don't.

"I saw a lot of friends, when they came home, that shit really got to them. For some of them, that's all they would talk about. They just kept fucking replaying the battle over and over, I mean even sometimes what they were telling wasn't even the same thing. The fuckin' battles just got mixed up. (He says this smiling and grinning.) We all knew what we were getting into until the firing began. Then it's all new shit. Sometimes it just lasted a few minutes, and sometimes it would last for weeks. No shit, I met guys over here who were fighting every fuckin' day for two months.

"It's not easy to get over, but you at least have to try. We are not going to hold your hand, but we will have your backs. Hey, if you are afraid to talk to anyone, talk to us. We work 24/7. Our ears are open, all fifty gazillion of us. We've got your back."

INSPIRATIONAL MESSAGE II

When you sacrifice your own learning opportunities in order to help others, you transcend the lesson you would have had to learned and create an accomplishment that far exceeds the primary lesson. For when you reach out to help others and sacrifice your time, energy, and being, it creates a wonderful opportunity for growth and understanding that cannot be equaled by a mere experience.

Chapter 20
FINDING ONE'S PURPOSE AFTER WAR

The reason we want to talk about this subject, Joe, is because many soldiers returning home wonder what they want to achieve in the next phase of their lives. Many have the same questions as other returning soldiers in past conflicts. Some of the statements we make might be broad, but they can definitely be applied to today's returning soldiers.

When a soldier returns from a war zone, he is apprehensive about getting back to a normal state of life. Therefore, sometimes returning to the civilian world from which he originally came but which he is not used to due to his military service can be difficult. During the time of service, things may have been very regulated with regard to expectations, and his actions were predetermined. However, in civilian life, he realizes that his freedom to make choices has been returned to him, which can sometimes cause stress and anxiety.

It's not necessarily the returning freedom that causes anxiety but just the switch from a regulated daily routine to civilian life, where there are multiple options that he alone can decide.

Some soldiers return home and continue to work for the military. For them, the transition will be easier than for those who directly return to civilian life and who are no longer obligated to follow the decisions of others.

The first thing that is necessary for a returning soldier in that situation is to get into a routine that his mind and body will be able to acclimate to. This will reset his internal functions and make the transition back to civilian life easier. Those who do not instigate a routine or who put this off will find it harder to acclimate between a conflict zone and the safety of their past civilian life.

When all the greetings have been made and people begin to settle down into their new civilian life, a question of purpose will begin to take hold in the forefront of their mind. Some may begin the transition by jumping into an activity or occupation right away but then later will begin to think that their choice may have been conceived too early. For others, it can happen much more quickly. It is a normal reaction to reevaluate one's life after accomplishing something that is so outside the norm of a day in, day out civilian life.

Some soldiers may equate their actions in a war zone to what they must accomplish in their new civilian life. Other times, these returning soldiers will slip back into the life they experienced before being involved in conflict. Each individual, depending on the surrounding circumstances, will make that decision when the time comes.

Before they actually leave the battlefield, some will begin to think about what they will do after their time in a conflict zone is over. While thinking of home during times of stress, they may reminisce about past occupations, relationships, and good times. They may seek the comfort of these thoughts during the time away from home and tell themselves that they will return to these things once they are relieved of their duties in the military.

It is important to realize that these decisions will be based on multiple factors, some conscious and others subconscious. Some soldiers will realize they wish to accomplish larger and more meaningful goals. Others will wish to return home, start families, and live what they consider to be normal lives. Each individual will think and decide how he wishes to proceed with his life. Some will follow friends and colleagues in directions they may take, while others will go off on their own or perhaps collaborate with family and friends back home.

All of these options will occur at some point in a returning soldier's mind. But other factors will also be brought into the decision-making process. These factors will be based on the experiences that the soldier was involved in while away from home. He may be affected by a higher state of awareness, such as the realization of how life can be very short and uncertain. People dwelling on this particular idea may wish to accomplish goals that others might see as impossible. Their fear of failure and disappointment is overtaken by the fact that they do not want to *waste time* on the Earth plane without taking the opportunity to experience new and wonderful things.

Some will seek out help in the decision-making process from fellow veterans, family members, and close friends. Others might have certain ideals and goals already set in their minds and will proceed on that path.

All of these actions will have common denominators within them. As any person coming of age thinks about what he wishes to accomplish in life, a returning soldier is much more acutely aware of this process due to the experiences he has just been a part of. So many are ready to go, right off the bat, while others may become burdened trying to decide what is best for them.

Start off with the core basis of who you want to be.

Ask yourself whether what you experienced is going to hold you back or propel you forward.

Take your newfound skills and use them to determine your future.

Don't let fear and inaction frighten you into not making a choice.

Reach out and help fellow soldiers in making their decisions.

Whatever choice you make is the right choice at that time.

Stay healthy physically, mentally, emotionally, and spiritually.

Take your new life in small pieces; otherwise, you may become overwhelmed.

It's not always easy, but that's okay.

"Joe, I just want to step in and tell you a few things that happened to me when I returned home. When I came home, there were lots of opportunities for me to work. I could've worked for my friend's father's business or started my own. I wanted to start out on my own and build something from scratch. I was lucky to have a lot of support from friends and family. They helped me research all the information I needed in order to start my own business. I had the backing, physically and emotionally, from loved ones. Joe, this is so important—to have others helping you achieve your goals.

"Some of my friends I had while in the service took a different route when they came home. They got caught up in the party scene and never settled down or thought about what they wanted to achieve in their lives.

"They all liked to talk a lot, but when it actually came down to doing the work, they would shrug it off. Some people you just can't help.

"What I learned is that you can do anything you want to. You might think you have limitations, but you don't. I really mean that just because it's hard doesn't mean it's impossible. If it doesn't work right away, try something else, but don't give up. You might not know what you truly want when you come home, but over time you might realize that you're achieving things that are very important to you in your life.

"So don't put all the stress on yourself at the beginning. It's not worth it—it's just not necessary. Life changes, and so will you. Good luck and God bless."

John, Army 2nd Battalion 162, World War II, Pacific

(I fought with the Army, Navy, Air Force, and Marines. But I belong to the Army—that was the service I was obligated to. We fought with the Marines in certain battles. I was involved with all the service branches just because we were all involved in that particular battle or area. We all work together, we all fight together. So when one of us says we fought with this group or that group, it may sound conflicting, but it's not to us. Sure, we had our differences, but when you're in battle, the only differences is us and them. Just before my discharge, I hooked up with a couple of guys from the Marines. We were all ready to go home, and one of the guys said to me, "How's it feel to be part of the Marines?" I said, "What are you talking about? I'm Army." And the Marine said, "You weren't back there—you fought like a Marine."

I laughed, and we went our separate ways. So just because you are affiliated with a certain branch of the military does not mean you don't fight with the other branches.)

Chapter 21
HOW HELPING OTHERS CAN HELP YOU HEAL

Joe, we want to talk about how soldiers can learn healing techniques to help them when they return home from their involvement in a war.

One of these techniques is the ability to help others achieve their goals in life. There are many different ways for returning soldiers to accomplish this. They can become involved in a group structure that advances the cause for many, or they can work one-on-one with those in need of a helping hand in order to enjoy and prosper in life.

One of the reasons this technique works so well is that when completing a tour of duty, a soldier will begin to think about the next stages of his life—what he wishes to accomplish, what he can bring to society, and how he can continue to grow as a person. Reaching out and helping others can help fill a void that may have been created while serving in a conflict area.

By helping others, the soldier is putting himself in the secondary position, and by doing this, he's sacrificing some of his time and energy in order to propel another's life goals. By making the sacrifice, the soldier is actually healing himself on many different levels. By sacrificing his time and energy in order to help another, the soldier's personal and spiritual growth will advance by leaps and bounds. It will help his development on many different levels. It will increase the veteran's speed of healing and reactivation into society.

Many times you've heard the expression "giving back." This is an example of how giving back can be used as a healing technique for someone who has experienced trauma in a war zone.

When one is focusing on helping another, he has a tendency not to fixate on his own problems. He is more focused on helping another through either relieving that person's pain and suffering or helping him on his journey toward creating a worthwhile life. Many times these efforts go unseen, but the effects have created a wonderful transition for both the soldier and the person he is helping.

Sometimes the soldier can partake in these activities on a part-time basis while going about his daily life. Other times, returning veterans will focus totally on an effort to help or change a particular situation. Examples of this include soldiers who give their time helping fellow veterans or working with disabled children or people who need help with educational disciplines.

The form of help comes in many different colors of the spectrum, but the giving is the most important part, for giving the time and energy is what creates the healing opportunity. Many times, soldiers returning home from a conflict zone will wonder how they can make something of their lives in order to balance the involvement that they might have partaken of where violence has occurred.

Today thousands of returning soldiers are coming home to an economy that is less than robust. They will have to make decisions about how to survive themselves as well as provide for their families. On top of that, they will have to deal with the underlying conditions that are part of acclimating to the civilian lifestyle.

There'll be many opportunities for returning soldiers to adjust their life paths. Many of the lessons they need to learn on the Earth plane will be entangled in the path they choose. Some lessons may become more direct, while others may take more time and patience in order to be accepted and learned. We would like to see the soldiers use the available opportunities to help one another and also help civilians who are in need.

They will have to make changes in how they think about helping others. By this, we mean that receiving a handout is not a bad thing. It is actually a complex exchange of energy. It is by no means short lived and will carry a positive flow throughout a person's life.

The soldier must realize that helping those in need is not a sign of weakness but a sign of great strength. He will need to focus on the fact that he is not showing pity toward an individual but is actually becoming actively involved in caring for someone other than himself.

Don't hold back your feelings when giving to others.

Don't get upset if others shun your efforts.

Don't think it'll be easy every time you extend a helping hand.

By helping others, you will achieve a great resource within your spirit.

Let giving be part of the new you.

Giving can be physical help, emotional support, and spiritual understanding.

Don't give just for the sake of giving. Give from your heart and the healing will magnify itself.

"My name is John, PFC. I wanted to give some perspective from where I am now. When I came home, I didn't want to deal with anyone. I didn't want to talk about the war, and I didn't want to hear about it or deal with anything. I liked to smoke, drink, and pass out. That was about it.

"Then one day I met this girl who wanted to help me get past some of the experiences that I'd thought had ruined my life. She wanted to help me understand what I'd gone through and how it was not my fault. At first I didn't give a shit, you know, I thought maybe it was just a piece of ass. But the more I talked with her, the more I realized that she was helping me on a deeper level.

"After a while, I started coming back out to the real world, getting involved in activities, watching sports, and just being more involved in life. If she had not taken the time to help me bridge this gap, I would've drank myself to death. No doubt, I was a fuckin' mess, man. She helped save my life.

"So what I'm trying to say is if someone reaches out to help you, take that hand. There's a lot to life, and you can lose out on a lot of opportunities by not getting help. On the flipside, I realized how important it was for me to accept her help.

"I tried talking to others who had similar experiences to mine. Some listened, some didn't, but I tried. It helped me a lot to try to help others. You don't realize that part of your body has been numbed by the drugs and alcohol. You forget that wonderful feeling, that great feeling you get when you help someone. It felt great that I wasn't constantly fixated on my own problems but was actually able to help someone else fix his.

"You can do a lot of good work, even if you don't feel up to it. It was a long, slow road for me, but it was worth it.

"Hey, give it a try. If you don't like it, fuck it. But you'll be very surprised. I'm glad I did.

"Tell everyone Joe Jackson said 'Hi.'"

(I'm not sure if John was his enlisted name, but he went by Joe.)

Chapter 22
HOW ANXIETY AND STRESS CAN BE DISRUPTIVE TO THE LEARNING PROCESS

Today we would like to discuss how anxiety and stress can be disruptive to the learning process. At times throughout people's lives, certain learning experiences can cause great stress and fear. These are the result of experiencing new challenges and not being able to digest them properly. When someone learns something for the first time, it will create emotional memories for that individual. If the event is joyous and happy, these memories will add to other similar memories and eventually will be looked back on with fondness. However, if these new learning experiences are traumatic, these events may stifle happy and joyous memories and take precedence over them.

You see, the trauma is being analyzed over and over by the mind in order to find relief. While a joyous memory might be enjoyed at the present moment and perhaps at a later date, the traumatic experience can be ongoing.

When an individual participates in a conflict zone or during war, dramatic experiences can be part of daily life. Even civilians in the war zone or those who are safe thousands of miles away can also experience traumatic events.

The more one enjoys the interaction with positive events and memories, the more a person's body will be able to flow through life with the expectations of looking forward to new experiences.

When a traumatic event occurs during the time of war and that memory is brought home, we see it often being relived over and over throughout the veteran's life. When this occurs, his ability to experience new life challenges is stunted. He is not able to fully experience new events in his life due to the traumatic memories.

One of the side effects of the mind analyzing these traumatic memories is chemical reactions that can affect the physical and emotional body. Many of you understand this as stress. There are different types of stress, depending on different situations and life experiences. We will not go into the different levels, as it can be complex at times. However, with military service and the stress that is involved during wartime, we can be more specific on how the body has to deal with it. In civilian life, there are times when traumatic events will occur within one's lifetime. Many times these events are uncontrollable and happen spontaneously. When we see traumatic events being created during the time of war, there are other problems that will occur due to this environment.

Soldiers may question why they decided to join a fight or perhaps a role in the military. Spouses and children may wonder why their love one is being put in harm's way. Soldiers may think that if they had not made certain decisions, they would not have experienced these dramatic events. They may blame themselves for becoming injured due to certain decisions they made. All this self-analysis creates additional stress that a civilian experiencing a traumatic event may not have to deal with.

Many times civilians will have more outlets to deal with the anxiety and stress that have accumulated due to a traumatic situation, while a soldier returning from war may have additional hurdles to jump in order to gain the help he needs.

When anxiety and stress take hold of one's life to the degree that decisions and the ability to function on a daily basis are challenged, one's ability to learn life lessons will be compromised. At times these life lessons will be misinterpreted and misunderstood due to the stress that the individual is suffering at the time. The stress will not have anything to do with the new event but will be a continuation of the past traumatic event.

An individual cannot grow fully and learn the experiences that he has to learn on the Earth plane if his life is chronically filled with anxiety and stress. It makes these life lessons much more difficult to comprehend and acquire. These new lessons are not assimilated into the person's whole the way they should be due to the outside influences of stress.

Do not relate new experiences with older traumatic events.

Try to separate your time of service from the events in your civilian life.

It is okay to have stress. There is a purpose for it, but there is no room for chronic stress.

Allow yourself to enjoy new experiences to the fullest.

If anxiety and fear cripple your ability to maintain happiness, seek out help—it's your right.

Leave fear and anxiety where they belong—in the past, with the traumatic event.

Don't bring the baggage of the past into your future, for you will have no room for the new experiences that might bring you great joy and more understanding of who you actually are.

"We all drank to get rid of those memories, but all that did was create new problems. I mean, we saw some incredible stuff—heads blown off, people walking around without limbs, that type of shit. It's not easy to forget something like that, but you have to—otherwise they own you. You're like the living dead. You're never going to remove those memories, but by accepting them and putting them in their place, you'll have a good start at a new life.

"Just remember, you don't have to live life scared of your shadow; you can come out into the light and enjoy yourself. Take it from us—we know you can do it. Give it a try, and if you don't like it, go back to the way you were. We are with you guys all the way. Stay strong—that's some tough shit you've been through. We know, we've been there. It ain't going to get easier until *you make* it easier. Shit, you can do it—you got through that crap the first time. Don't take no for an answer in getting help; hell, be a persistent bastard. It's your life; you have a right to be happy. We can help you to some degree, but you have to take control of your own life. That's how it works. Good luck and God bless."

James, Marine Corps

("My friends called me Jimmy. I had red hair and a wide grin. From Nebraska, I have two kids living in the States. They're grown now. I'm still around keeping an eye on them. Saw lots of action in Southeast Asia. Left many friends there, too—what a shame. Some are with me, some are still on your level. 'Ooh-rah' to my buddies!")

Chapter 23
POW/MIA

Prisoners of War

Joe, when it comes to prisoners of war, we pay special attention to their needs, wants, and desires. We realize that these needs might not be the same needs that the particular soldier expects at the time. By this, we mean that we can see the bigger picture from our side and know how to direct our energy in order to support the soldier who has been captured during a conflict.

Many times soldiers will act out due to the fear that they are isolated from their spiritual selves. Some might say, "God has forgotten about me." But at no time have his spiritual brothers in arms left his side. Some soldiers under extreme circumstances may be able to sense us around them. Others have had discussions with us concerning the situation. In extreme situations, we are allowed to intervene in that soldier's energy in order to bring strength and physical abundance, for that soldier's physical and psychological makeup might have been disrupted by the reality of the situation to the point where it will affect future plans for his spiritual growth.

These are exceptional cases and are implemented depending on the action of the soldier, the situation, and the likely outcome if our intervention is not called into action. We realize that this may cause some confusion as to why we can interact with some soldiers and not others, but it is difficult for you on the Earth plane to understand the perspective we are seeing. Some situations that are being played out have been manipulated by outside sources, and they need to be put back on track. These sources may not have been a part of the equation of the learning experience of the battle, the capture, and the eventual outcome.

The sources we speak of are high influences that may not have the best intentions in getting involved in the guidance of the human spirit. Sometimes outside entities will try to influence situations and can corrupt preplanned outcomes. So during these times, we are allowed to step forward and reset the motions that have been planned out.

We understand the worry, concern, and suffering that affect the loved ones and colleagues of the soldier who has become a prisoner of war. We work closely with these other individuals as well as the soldier. If the soldier returns home, he will need the support of his family and friends in order to begin the healing process on the Earth plane. So we closely watch over all who are affected by the current situation.

We have teams of guides who specialize in the oversight of prisoners of war and their families for they experience certain events that other soldiers will not be exposed to. Their families will experience certain stresses that other military families will not. So these particular guides are trained to work in this specific field. Many of these guides are past POWs who never returned home. They have the insight and new perspective on how to deal with the uncertainties the soldier faces as well as those faced by his family and loved ones.

We all work together with all the soldiers and families, but special teams are broken down for specific situations and specific healing duties. Some groups are better trained to bring healing to the psychologically injured, while other teams have great insight and bring inspiration and motivation to physically injured soldiers. Our POW teams will work with the soldier throughout his captivity as well as when he is reunited with his family. In the event that the prisoner of war is not returned to his family and crosses over to our side, he is met by the special team that will help him acclimate to his new spiritual life.

This team will show him the reasons for his crossing over, the events that surround his situation, and how his life has affected others in a positive way. Most of these things cannot be seen from the Earth plane's perspective but only once the soldier has reached our side.

He is comforted, supported, and safe. His needs are taken care of, and special focus is given to family and friends he has left behind. There is a whole mechanism that takes place when this situation occurs, and this is something we may expand upon in new writings.

The act of being under the control of others can be quite stressful. The unknowing, the fear, and the physical pressure placed on the soldier will at times cause extreme posttraumatic stress syndrome. While under the control of an enemy combatant, the soldier feels the most vulnerable. This is why we watch over him closely—because this is when he is more open to outside influences that are not necessary.

Soldiers who have control of other soldiers have their own concerns and stresses. While some may relish the position of authority to create stress, fear, and pain in the lives of others, this is not the case with many of the military personnel who oversee prisoners of war. When torture, both physical and mental, occurs, there are controlling soldiers who become very stressed and who begin to show signs similar to those who experience posttraumatic stress syndrome.

For the soldiers begin to question their own essence regarding how they can cause pain and suffering to an individual who is not able to defend himself. They will question what type of human being they are when they can manipulate a situation in order to bring great trauma to an individual who is in their care. When they are not on duty, they will begin to analyze the actions they have taken. This will continue for many after the conflict is over and they have returned to civilian life. These thoughts will be very deep within their psyche, as they are not easily talked about in an open forum. There are few who can understand the feelings they are experiencing, and therefore many of these silent injuries are carried with the soldiers throughout their lives.

It is not often talked about how a soldier feels about his obligation in overseeing a captured enemy. For you must remember that in conflict, one's enemy is still a human being. We have seen this throughout the ages, and it is common to all humans. It is something that is shared because we are all spiritual beings. Even though you come from different cultures or countries in different time periods, you are all spiritual beings who have to answer questions about your own actions.

All who are involved in the control of others in a prisoner-of-war situation are asked to make significant decisions that will affect the growth of that soldier's spiritual path. There are great learning opportunities in these situations. From the prisoner of war to his captor, each will have opportunities to grow or to take a step back in his soul's learning process. By being part of this group, you have made a courageous choice, for you will be given many opportunities to adjust your soul's growth.

It takes much courage to put oneself in the situation. There are so many times and so many decisions that have to be made that the prisoner-of-war circumstance is an accelerated learning curve. You can take great strides in your growth as a spiritual being, but you also can take great falls and create major hurdles in your life growth to come.

Some individuals are placed in the situation in order to create chaos—conflict in circumstances in which lessons can be learned. These individuals may seem at times to be of a lower level of spirit but actually have taken on the personality of ignorance in order to help the soldier with his learning opportunities. These individuals take a great chance when assuming this responsibility, as it may corrupt their own learning abilities and set them back. To take on this responsibility, they are usually risking their own spiritual growth. In these cases, many of these people have come forward to take responsibility in order to make up for past mistakes.

Any outside influences within the situations are strictly controlled, but some outside influences do make their way in under concealment. This is where we have to step in and give assistance to a soldier or situation in order for the whole learning experience to get back on track.

We would now like to give you some insight from soldiers who have been part of the prisoner-of-war experience. These insights come from the perspective of being on our side and may be confusing to some of you who are still looking at it from the limited perspective of the Earth plane. Some of these comments are directed to future POWs.

Realize that the situation herein is meant to be.
Don't take it personally—there are other factors at play.
We watch over you every minute of the day.
We hear your prayers, your suffering, and your pleas for assistance.
We need you to realize that there are others who are working on your behalf.
However the situation plays out, it will be a learning experience.
Helping a fellow POW can be healing in itself.

Many people feel trapped and suffer in the civilian world, and these characteristics can be similar to a POW's experience. So for the POW who is returning home to interact in the civilian world with people who are in need, it is as if you are helping a fellow soldier. On the spiritual level, you will help bring healing to that civilian, and that, in the bigger picture, would be like bringing healing to a fellow soldier in arms.

Joe, some of us made it home to our families and friends, while others came directly to our side. We are satisfied with our own outcomes. The questions that some of us had when we reached this side have been explained and experienced through working with others who are still alive on the Earth plane. We see why certain situations happened and how we played a direct role in them. It is very honorable to have been a part of the prisoner-of-war experience, as many humans will not take on this responsibility or opportunity for growth. It is one aspect of the human experience that is a challenge that many entities would not take.

We are at peace with ourselves, and we want to tell the families that are still on the Earth plane to take care of themselves, to bring healing to others, and that we are still connected to you and will remain so until it is your time to join us here on our side.

Missing in Action

Joe, we realize that you wanted to mention the issue of soldiers missing in action. We realize that this topic is very sensitive for many civilians as well as veterans. The reason for this is because of the unknown. When friends and families do not know where their loved one is and are not sure if he is suffering, it can bring great stress and anxiety to them. Current soldiers have their own worries and fears that their colleagues are not accounted for, as the same fate could happen to them. These worries can cause the mind to create its own ending to a situation that has not resolved itself.

There are many facets to the MIA issue. What we would like to talk about is how the individual who was missing in action is always connected to his fellow soldiers. Many of these soldiers have made it to our side, even though they have not been recognized as having given their lives during a conflict or battle. We realize that the criteria for MIAs raise many questions.

The main idea we wish for you to understand is that no one is left alone. They are always surrounded with peace, healing, and comfort. When a soldier first becomes missing in action and survives the conflict or interaction he has had with an enemy combatant, he is placed with a team of specialists from our side. This team attempts to bring calmness, guidance, and spiritual connection to him. This team will work with this particular soldier until it is his time to return to his homeland or return to his real home—the spirit world.

Many times MIAs are recorded due to the fact that a soldier's body could not be recovered. There are various reasons for this, and we will not be referring to them right now. But for the families and loved ones who wish to know about the condition of the particular soldier who became missing in action, he is safe. He has crossed back home to our side, where he was greeted by fellow soldiers, departed family members, and old friends.

He is in an area of enlightenment and has a new perspective on the role he played within the military and the role he played on the Earth plane. He will continue with his soul's growth and will help others make the transition from the Earth plane to the spiritual realm.

To the children of MIAs, we wish to inform you that your parent has made a great sacrifice, not only for his fellow soldiers but also for others who will learn great lessons through his passing. Some will learn the power of prayer, the power of continuing hope, and the realization that they will be reunited with their loved one in the future. Others will realize the importance of life itself. Many times people relate to the phrase "life is short." People associated with MIAs can relate to this expression very strongly.

So we wish to lift some of the burden that you may currently be experiencing if you love someone who has been lost. He is not alone. He is at peace in a place that is indescribable to any of you. His energy and spirit create the love and compassion that all of you feel on a daily basis.

We have the ability to interact with you on the Earth plane in order to bring you relief from your burdens and worries. We take this responsibility very seriously and do our best to live up to these high standards. You may think that we are missing in action, but it's ironic that we are right in the middle of the action, working with you every day and helping you to understand the concept that we are all connected and that we will always be together.

Chapter 24
DEALING WITH INJURIES

Joe, dealing with injuries for any human being is a difficult path to choose. Before one arrives on the Earth plane, certain decisions are made, and one of these is what life lessons you wish to experience. Some souls have chosen to arrive on the Earth plane in what some people would say would be a less optimal physical condition.

For others, a decision has been made that somewhere along their life's path, they would accept a disturbance to the physical body. The conscious mind, once on the Earth plane, does not remember these decisions that have been made on a soul level. We do not want individuals to try to analyze whether they have brought these conditions upon themselves. Some have made plans to have these physical limitations, while others gain them along the way for various reasons. For the purpose of this book, we will not expand into those other reasons, as we wish to stay focused to the subject.

When a soldier goes off to war, there is always the possibility of injury and death. As that soldier comes face to face with the brutalities of conflict, those possibilities increase and can alter the way the soldier begins to accept the situation. At one point, a soldier may be robust in his enthusiasm to partake in a battle, but once he has seen the carnage and loss of life and limb, he may begin to second-guess why he is in that particular situation.

When the individual witnesses the effects of war, he begins to think about how an injury would affect his life. Some say they would rather die than to come home with a physically disabling condition. Others would just be happy to come home alive.

What we see and understand is that a soldier will at times accept the injury that has befallen him. For some, the acceptance will be immediate, and he will try to move forward with his life. These soldiers understand that the experience of life itself is too important to give up on the opportunity for growth and happiness. They will seek out opportunities and participate with family and friends and will continue to grow and learn.

Other soldiers will direct their attention to themselves. They will not allow outside influences to help them understand what has happened and what possibilities are available for the future. They believe that the lack of a perfect physical body in itself has diminished them as a person. They believe an individual who has lost limbs or the ability to communicate is less of a person than one who has full physical capability.

The way the soldier reacts to his injury or to that of a fellow soldier's injury depends upon the state of mind of that soldier before he goes into battle. If he has an attitude that no matter what condition the physical body is in when he returns, that his essence—his true self—will still be intact, the reaction will be positive.

What many individuals do not understand is that having a physical or psychological injury will in fact help others grow and experience compassion. What the soldier has done is forfeited part of his physical being in order to help others learn and grow on this spiritual path. This is an extremely high level of giving. For one to take on this teaching lesson for the sake of others shows a level of enlightenment and awareness that is not seen by most humans.

So those who think these injuries are just a physical disturbance to the person's being are missing the larger picture. For we can see on the other side what role these injured soldiers play. These soldiers will interact with other soldiers and civilians and will bring about major changes in these individuals' lives. The soldier may or may not have a conscious awareness of the positive change that he has on others.

Some will learn this as they continue to grow on the Earth plane, while others may never understand the position they have taken. We want to let you know that there is a reason for a particular injury or suffering that you may not understand until you arrive on the other side.

However, we are taking this opportunity to give you the insight into the background on how this works. Some individuals will gain insight from this knowledge and use it for positive growth, others may not understand the whole concept that we are trying to explain, and some will even discard it outright.

There is a common concept that many people have heard, that things happen for a reason. This is actually an example of the situation that has taken place for a true reason. We know it's difficult for a soldier to try to understand why his legs are no longer part of the physical body and that it's related to some higher cause. But it is our job to pass on the information to him that this is indeed part of a larger cause.

If a soldier has been injured to the brink of death and is not physically capable of caring for himself, he will have individuals who care for him and, by doing so, will learn new levels of love and awareness. These are great learning lessons, and some of these lessons can only be learned through what you call a tragic situation such as an injury to a soldier during war.

There are many different levels of injuries due to the many different types of individuals who may need different types of lessons. On the physical side, soldiers may say that different injuries are caused by different devices and different situations. But that is the individual soldier's limited perspective, for he cannot see the larger picture that is in play from his position on the Earth plane.

While many injuries are physical in nature, soldiers for millennia have also suffered psychological and silent injuries. These injuries may not have any obvious characteristics but can be just as immobilizing as physical ones. Many civilians and even some soldiers cannot understand the concept of an unseen injury. This in itself adds to the injury in the people who have to deal with it. The nonacceptance of the injury by others can bring emotional stress and anxiety that are not necessary to the individual.

This is why it is important for fellow veterans to support one another. If one veteran does not understand or accept some of these silent injuries and "calls" a soldiers on them, it can have a devastating effect, for it is harder to hear this from a fellow veteran than a civilian. A veteran is supposed to be able to rely on another veteran—a soldier is supposed to have another soldier's back. When a veteran does not support another veteran, especially when there is an injury, this hits at the core of the brotherhood.

By helping your fellow soldiers during the time of war and accepting their injuries back in the civilian world, you will have made the choice in the acceptance of another being, for you will realize that a person is not just the physical structure that you can touch and visualize. The real person is the unseen force that is capable of love, courage, and compassion.

This is important for the veteran to understand when it comes to dealing with fellow soldiers who have been injured. If one has difficulty dealing with soldiers because of one's own insecurities, then you, too, share in a level of injury that would be considered silent. Do not judge yourself—just be aware that you, too, have been injured.

For those who are incapacitated to the level of unconsciousness, we have a direct line of communication with you. The reason we state this is so fellow soldiers and loved ones understand that we are working with those soldiers who are currently in the state of coma. We have not left their bedside, and we have not abandoned them. We are always connected to them, as we are always connected to all of you.

We have ways of contacting them directly, even though they do not respond to natural stimulus in your physical world. We can bring healing and compassion to them on a spiritual level, which will bring them comfort and understanding. There are soldiers on our side who specialize in dealing with wounded soldiers on the physical plane. They act as intermediaries in channeling information back and forth between the two spirits.

Do not despair if an injury has befallen you due to your service in the military. You have accepted the challenge that you have been asked to take on and have learned at a higher level how to teach others with the sacrifice you have made.

Do not despair over your injury.
There is a greater good that will come out of your injury.
You are helping teach others due to your injury.
We are watching over all the injured.
Silent injuries are as real as physical ones.
We work directly with unconscious and mentally injured individuals.
Don't wish for death over your injury. There are more opportunities for growth.

"Joe, my name's David. I had an injury to the left side of my body that left me paralyzed from the waist down. They took me off on a stretcher to a field hospital and then transported me back to the States a few months later. They say my spine was cut, something like that. All I knew was that I couldn't feel anything from my hips down.

"I was happy to be home and out of pain from what originally happened. But between the time I was injured and when I returned to the States, I went through a whole shitload of mental games. I couldn't comprehend the fact that I would not walk again. Frankly, it just pissed me off and at other times caused me to go into depression. I kept asking myself, 'Why the fuck did this happen to me? This shit can't be real, it can't be happening to me.'

But then you wake up one day and realize that it has happened to you and that you have two choices.

"You can go back in denial as you're crawling along the floor, or you can get the fuck up and begin to take control of your new life. You see, it's your decision. Life doesn't give a shit if you stay on the floor. But I gave a shit and didn't want to stay on that floor for the rest of my life. Now, some guys are so down that they don't have the strength to get up off the floor. This is where the help of others is needed. And I'm talking about a whole group of others, including nurses, counselors, family members, and brother soldiers. They must all help this guy get to a level where he can start helping himself. But the worst thing is if this guy wants to get off the floor and no one's there who wants to help him—that's just a damn shame. So many of you will lose the opportunity to grow by not helping out that person.

"Some others will just want to go home and not think about it. They'll just let time slip away and watch the years go by without taking an active role in who they are and where they want to go. The opportunities are endless. We have people who have taught, even though they were paralyzed from the freaking neck down. Their mind was still active, and they had the ability to talk and to teach other individuals.

"We have a guy over here who can play the guitar with his teeth, and no, it's not Jimi Hendrix. Jimmy's hanging out with some brothers right now, getting it on, if you know what I mean. He's a scream. He just likes to hang out and jam and make music. He taught a lot of folks how to appreciate the sounds and vibration of music. You have no idea how many souls he has helped heal with that tool you call music.

"So what I'm saying is take control of your life, no matter your physical or mental condition, and decide to move forward and create something with your life. I'm not talking about building a house or starting a business, although some will do that, but even something as simple as giving someone else the opportunity to care for you is creating something with your new life.

"Infantry, mother fucker, Ooh-rah!"

Chapter 25
WHY DID I GO TO WAR?

Joe, in the concept of war, there are two outstanding principles that we want to mention to you. We have taken a look at why conflicts take place, but we want to answer your question as to why an individual would want to become involved in such a serious confrontation as war.

It is our understanding that people question the reasons for getting involved in a conflict, especially after coming face to face with the dire consequences of that decision. Many times the idea of going into battle can be one of excitement and adventure, while the reality of being involved in a conflict can be far from those ideals.

Individuals will have similar reasons for joining a conflict. Some of these reasons may be to protect their homeland, protect their family, or protect their personal interests. Others may feel an obligation to help their fellow neighbors or countrymen. These individuals feel as if they need to be part of the bigger picture, to be part of a nation, or to be part of a cause. They wish to join in the conflict for personal reasons that are shared among many. This is where you will see a large group of people signing up to become involved in a short period of time.

Some people see it as a career to be honored and exercised. Some individuals believe the employment of the soldier is a job with security—a place for possible advancement up the employment ladder. They look at it as a job, as opposed to someone who has join the military for reasons we had stated above, such as to become involved in a group cause.

Many people believe that joining a group of armed members and going to far-off places will enable them to move away from the simplistic form of life they're currently residing in. They believe this is their opportunity to see other cultures and other parts of the world. The thought of becoming directly involved in combat is secondary to the thought of living an adventure. These people will also question themselves if they are put in a position in which interaction with others escalates to a violent stage. Some will accept this as part of the larger adventurous energy that they possess, while others will question themselves once again as to why they made such decision to leave the comfort and security of their own home.

Some others become involved because they are drawn into the conflict involuntarily. These individuals have the most difficult time reasoning why their lives have become involved in something so huge without their direct approval. They cannot make the connection between their involvement in the cause and the result that is trying to be achieved by the military or the leaders of the conflict.

We have seen that many times the soldier will question his reason for joining a particular conflict after he has become involved in situations that brought him into harm's way. He asks himself why he would put himself in danger of being killed or permanently disabled for a cause that does not immediately affect his family or neighbors.

This is a natural reaction to coming face to face with one's own mortality. He realizes that the decisions he has made have caused him to be at this point in his life—that those decisions are the reasons why his life is in jeopardy. This is the beginning of the questions that an individual poses to himself on many different levels. Some may seem to understand the reasons why they have join such a conflict, while others will fold it into many psychological ways in order to handle the situation.

When the conflict continues over a long period of time and the soldier's involvement continues with no end in sight, these questions become larger in his mind. These questions are brought up in the subconscious as well as periodically in his everyday thinking. This is where self-judgment begins—blaming himself for putting himself in this situation. The soldier will become his own worst judge for causing the pain and suffering he is enduring throughout the time of his involvement in the conflict.

These questions will follow the soldier after he leaves the conflict area and returns to his homeland. If the soldier has been in a combat situation or has been wounded, these questions will remain in the forefront of his thoughts. Many times this basic question will be added to other questions concerning actions he has taken while involved in the conflict. If he has killed or has witnessed horrendous acts of violence, he will come back to the question of why he decided to go to war, for if he had not made that decision, he would not have to deal with the memories in his mind of the conflict.

For those who were involuntarily brought into the conflict, anger builds as to why they were forced to witness and be involved in such atrocities that occurred during the time of war. They become angry at the powers that be who wanted or made them become involved in the conflict in the first place. Not only must they deal with their actions once they were involved in the conflict, but they blame those who got them involved in the first place. This adds to the burden and stress of the soldier when he arrives home.

Some soldiers will question their motives while in conflict, some of them sensing that they tricked themselves into believing what they were doing was for the best. They've become despondent that their actions have been manipulated by others and that they've been used. This also brings up anger that the leaders of certain conflicts have used the soldier's sense of loyalty for their own selfish reasons. The soldier realizes that what he is doing is not what he signed up for or the reason he joined; rather, the leaders of the conflict have chosen him as a pawn in a larger game of conflict.

Many times soldiers are very happy for the opportunity to have served their fellow man in combat. They enjoy the camaraderie of their fellow soldiers and the special memories that they can only share due to their involvement in a particular situation. Their growth as both humans and spiritual beings is affected by their involvement in a particular conflict. If they believe that they are helping a cause and they see some of the good acts that happen inside the arena of war, they are reassured that they themselves are strong spiritual beings.

Examples of this may include saving a young child in a war zone, protecting civilians, bringing help and relief to fellow soldiers, and being able to show compassion inside a chaotic, violent situation. These people can take these small acts of compassion and feelings with them when they return to their home and can help others in relieving the pain they have endured while in conflict.

This is why it is very important for fellow soldiers to help each other in understanding the role they have played in a war zone. Civilians can also point out some of these simple acts that the soldier has been involved in and how he has brought healing, comfort, and serenity to others while in the combat situation. While some soldiers will judge themselves in a negative way for their actions toward others, it is important for them to realize that some of their other actions have been reflected positively onto others while serving in a conflict. It is important to point out these positive interactions so as to help the healing process.

Your decision to become involved was made in the past.
You could not have predicted the experiences you were involved in.
You had honorable intentions when you decided to become involved.
Your perspective has now changed—so should your expectations.

Focus on the good that you have provided; even the slightest smile or handshake can have a magnificent effect on an individual. Do not believe that no good at all has come from your service. There are many instances of you bringing peace and comfort that you will not even realize until you reach our side. Remember this.

Chapter 26
FEELING GUILTY, FEELING NOTHING

When soldiers are involved in a conflict situation and lives are lost, there will always be a degree of guilt concerning the fairness of who dies and who gets to live. When soldiers train and live in close quarters for certain periods of time, they become much more aware of the people around them. Some may call this a bonding, while others may call it a realization of their fellow soldiers as human beings. They are not just instruments of war but actually have lives, families, and loved ones who are connected to them.

Many times specialized groups will be especially close, as they may experience certain missions with the same group of people. Each person may specialize to a certain degree in a different aspect of war, but together as a group they function as one unit. Even though some soldiers may be on an individual mission or perhaps with only a small group, they still consider themselves part of a larger group or unit. The longer the soldier serves with others, the closer they may become to each other. Many times we see soldiers who have experienced war return to civilian life and continue to be close friends with others they have served with in the past. There is a special connection that individuals share when going through similar experiences at the same time. We see this in civilian life, but it is much more acute during the interaction of war.

When an individual soldier is killed in action and it is witnessed by his fellow soldiers, it can create emotional stress throughout the unit. At first, if the situation is chaotic, the response from the soldiers may be muted as they concentrate on the matter at hand. When the smoke clears and the injured and dead are retrieved and the unit returns to a safe area, individual soldiers' emotions may become more active. It is often during this downtime when recollection of the death of a fellow soldier slips into the conscious mind of the remaining soldiers.

This is where questions begin to come out concerning the events that led up to the soldier being killed. Analysis of the situation will go from the basic action that has occurred to possible prevention of the death. Depending on the situation, a soldier's death may have been prevented, and at other times it was inevitable. Fellow soldiers who experienced this loss firsthand will begin to ask themselves why their friend died and not them. They will rationalize that they were both involved in the same conflict at the same time, so why didn't they die as well? Other times, fellow veterans and soldiers who are not in the conflict zone, when learning of the death of a fellow soldier, will be reminded of times when they served in a war zone and will begin to wonder why they have survived while some of their colleagues perished.

Once again, self-judgment will overtake the analysis of the situation, and one may begin to feel guilty about still being alive.

Many times soldiers will rationalize this guilt on many different levels. Some will say, "It should have been me," some will say, "It was my time," and others may ask, "Why some and not others?"

This situational guilt can sometimes last a lifetime for some individuals as they manipulate the experience over and over, tormenting themselves and at the same time feeling a sense of relief from these self-destructive thoughts. Other soldiers and veterans may have brief episodes of guilt come and go throughout their involvement in a conflict zone, but when returning to civilian life may only briefly experience the same feelings.

Some individuals will be emotionally scarred to the point of shutting down certain emotions. It's as if they get burned out about trying to understand the death of a colleague. Their emotions become numb in order to stop the pain they are feeling from their own analysis of the passing of a fellow soldier.

Some of these soldiers take this numbness as not caring about the loss of a fellow soldier. They believe they are less of a person for not caring about a fellow human being who had a family and children back home.

Any emotional response to the death of the soldier creates chemical and physical reactions within the body that may be experienced differently from individual to individual.

Some soldiers are meant to die in combat. Their deaths have meaning, even though others may not understand it at the present time.

Some soldiers are meant to witness the passing of a fellow soldier in order to achieve the foundation of future learning experiences.

There are reasons why things happen that you will never understand on the Earth plane.

Carrying guilt and emotional stress for a long period of time will disrupt future learning experiences for each individual.

We don't mind you missing us, but don't screw up the rest of your life.

Let go of the baggage you carry—it's not worth it. We see this from the other side.

We hear your prayers and conversation but want you to enjoy your life, so move on, soldier.

Many times soldiers resist the opportunity to accept the situation and move forward in their lives. This is unsettling to us, for the opportunity to move forward after being involved in a violent situation is very important in the learning process. Some will be so overwhelmed that they will not be able to move forward, and these individuals may experience this in order for others to learn about compassion and care. However, many soldiers who have the opportunity to move forward do not take advantage of others' generosity, caring, and empathy, and thus do a disservice to those helping people who also have a learning opportunity in helping you return to being a stable, functioning human being.

As we have said before and will say again: Let it go, let it go.

INSPIRATIONAL MESSAGE III

Injuries, both silent and physical, can be extremely powerful sources of opportunities. These opportunities are limited to a few, and therefore the energy surrounding them magnifies the potential for positive growth. The lessons learned by both the injured and those who come in contact with them are of special significance. They are unique and cannot be experienced in any other form. Your ability to create love and compassion is at its highest during these times of affliction.

Chapter 27
AS A CIVILIAN, HOW CAN I TALK TO A COMBAT SOLDIER WHEN HE COMES HOME?

Many times when a soldier returns home after being involved in a conflict zone, he is greeted by family and friends who at times are not sure who he is. The family and friends, who have never been in a conflict zone, have read about the events of previous wars, have talked to other veterans about their experiences, and at times may have many questions to ask their loved one.

Some are afraid to ask specific questions about the possible involvement of their loved one in the killing of other humans for fear of upsetting the returning soldier. Others want to share the intimacy of the details that their love one has experienced.

The interactions with family, friends, and fellow veterans might be quite different for various reasons. A veteran who has seen past combat and has experienced similar feelings when returning to the civilian world will give time and space to the returning soldier to allow him to acclimate to civilian life.

However, as we often see, family members who are in direct contact with the returning soldier on a daily basis might not be able to afford to give time and space due to the interaction of being a family. Some spouses may wish to ask personal questions but at times have been told to hold off. It is difficult for them to try to communicate with their loved one while also having to censor some of the things they say.

Throughout the history of war, these emotions that are introduced when soldiers return home have stayed the same. Before modern communications, civilians at home would witness returning injured soldiers who would speak of battles they participated in. So when their spouse returned home, they knew some of the intimate details of the war.

Today's communication is much more modern and instantaneous. Family and loved ones can get up-to-date news and even view the active battle scene. However, being able to view war at a distance is different from having actually participated in it.

Some spouses take it upon themselves to believe that they're entitled to every piece of the emotion that the returning soldier has experienced. However, the returning soldier might not have the ability to explain certain events or his feelings. He may still be readjusting to activities he had to participate in that caused pain and suffering to fellow human beings. As time goes on and the soldier begins to acclimate back to civilian life, he will begin to process the actions he was involved in and may be able to communicate these to civilians with a better perspective.

It is important for the civilian to realize that the returning soldier's most valuable asset is just being home. The simple things in life are much more appreciated when returning home, and the indulgence of the simple things is paramount to the returning soldier. Complex issues, emotions, and communications about his involvement in the war can wait, as the enjoyment of being home in a safe environment is the most precious thing the soldier seeks.

Many times friends and family will approach the soldier and begin to ask personal, in-depth questions about his involvement in the war. In times past, civilians would not approach the returning soldier, as they learned very early on that many veterans did not wish to speak of the events they had been a part of.

When the civilian begins to ask personal questions about a soldier's involvement in the violence of war, he may wish to try to answer these truthfully and respectfully. However, many times it is quite a burden to put on his shoulders. The soldier does not want to be disrespectful to the civilian who seeks out the answers, but the soldier realizes that the questions are much more complex than the civilian who was asking them realizes. A simple question about involvement in a particular area in a conflict zone might have multiple answers dealing with multiple situations that cannot be explained easily in a short conversation.

This might be a time when you might experience a soldier giving a short, abrupt answer to one of your questions. It is not that he doesn't wish to answer fully—it's just that he believes that you will not be able to fully accept the complexity of the situation.

Complex questions cannot be answered in small talk.

Don't ask us if we've killed anyone. That's very personal.

Ask us about common themes such as living conditions, food, and environment.

We will want to tell you of more personal experiences, but you might have to wait some time.

Don't ask us about our feelings right away because we are still trying to figure them out.

We can't help what we have experienced and are sometimes afraid that we will be judged.

Ask us about our friends and fellow soldiers in the unit. This will show how we are bound to our fellow soldiers.

I know I have to mow the lawn, but some days I might be preoccupied with things from the war.

Don't take it personally—just give me space. Sometimes I need to be alone.

The kids are fine. They'll understand as they get older.

Don't be angry at the condition of my body. Just be happy that I am home safe.

If you want to know the truth, I will tell you, but don't try to change it to make it sound okay.

It happened, it's over, let's move on.

Chapter 28

HOW DO I TELL MY FAMILY AND OTHERS ABOUT WHAT I HAVE EXPERIENCED?

Trying to explain one's experiences in a conflict zone to others who have never experienced such situations can be extraordinarily difficult and complex. One first has to realize and analyze one's own experience in one's own mind before one can even contemplate trying to explain it to an outsider. Many times this analysis and judgment of one's own activities during the time of war can come into conflict when one is questioned directly about one's involvement.

Some of the experiences that must be explained do not have easy explanations. The actions taken and experienced may be discussed in a straightforward way, but the reasons for some of these actions are much more complex.

A person may approach the subject and deal with it directly, telling exactly what happened to him when he was involved in the situation that caused pain and suffering. He may relate details of specific missions he was involved in that brought about death to other people. He may even explain some of his emotions during the situations. But this might not be the total answer.

Many will not be able to describe the experiences they have participated in during the war for fear of being judged for their actions. They will think, and rightly so at times, that people will judge them as a certain type human being, depending on their actions inside a war zone.

This should not be the case. One should be able to explain in detail one's experiences under extreme stress that have occurred in a conflict area without having to fear someone else's judgment.

This is often why we see veterans talking to other veterans about their experiences. It is not only because they share common experiences, but they also feel that other veterans will be less judgmental toward them. They feel that there is greater trust and more of a bond between fellow soldiers than between a soldier and a civilian. This is one of the main reasons why this book is being written—to help soldiers get guidance from fellow veterans.

Soldiers will explain their experiences to different people in different ways. What is told to a close friend or colleague may be different from what is told to an acquaintance or neighbor. The degree of the experience will also shift, depending on who is receiving the information. The soldier will decide who will get the full experience and who will get an abridged version.

When it comes to explaining one's experiences in a conflict zone to a family member, many of these problems occur to a higher degree. The soldier wanting to tell his spouse about his experiences may be in conflict, as the spouse may be his best friend but at the same time there's a fear of losing that closeness if the soldier's actions are judged. At times the soldier will become tormented about how much information to release to a loved one. This also can bring about guilt, which can compromise a soldier's acclimation back into civilian life.

It is important for family members to realize this problem. Is important to accept your partner the way he is—even the changed personality that may exist when he returns home—for he has lived life and experienced things at an accelerated rate that the soldier himself is still trying to comprehend. And when brought into a relationship, it's difficult and complex to work out certain problems when the returning soldier is still trying to figure out his own experiences.

When children are involved and ask questions about a parent's involvement in a war, a different set of standards is needed in order to facilitate a proper answer. A returning soldier may wish to protect his children from the visual pain and suffering that he may bring to them if he explains in detail some of the events that occurred in the war zone. It is not that the soldier wishes to hide these events from his child, but he may want to protect the child from undue stress.

If the children are of an older age, more information can be given to them, depending on their maturity. Each parent must judge the maturity of his own children in deciding how much information should be shared with them. Children in modern times have access to more information about a particular war and may actually experience visual aspects of that war, while in the past children were informed of conflicts through storytelling.

A returning soldier parent may feel more open to sharing his feelings and experiences with a mature child, as he feels that there is less chance of that child being judgmental of him. Many times the soldier will trust his feelings more with the child than with an adult, as adults are quicker to judge others.

Sometimes in past wars, soldier parents did not talk about their experiences at all to civilians or family members. This was the norm during those specific times. Soldiers must deal with the current cultural makeup that welcomes them when they come home. During the history of conflict, soldiers have been greeted back home in a variety of ways, including celebrations and disdain. These welcoming situations will have an effect on how a soldier relates his experiences to his friends, family, and especially children.

It seems at times that children are more adaptable to experiences that they learn. However, when a parent is involved in a war zone, it brings about many emotional feelings on different levels for children. A soldier parent can explain his experiences to children in a way as to not upset them and may continue to relay his experiences as the children become adults. Explaining any process to children is different from explaining a process to adults. This should also be the case when relaying the details of a war experience to children.

Children whose parents have been injured face many additional problems in dealing with the parent who has been in a war zone. The complexity of the experience for them is quite acute as they witness the physical trauma that the parent has been involved in. At times, it may be necessary to tell the children exactly what happened to the parent and why their loved one was injured. It is also very important to interact with the children and let them know that they are still loved and that the soldier is still their parent.

If the injury is a physical disability, this may be more easily accomplished than if there is trauma to the brain. If the injury causes a lack of communication skills on the part of the returning soldier, a fellow family member must discuss the situation with the children in order to relieve the suffering that the children will experience. Constant reinforcement that the children's parent is still their parent and still loves them very much is vital to the mental health of the child.

The course of action that the soldier goes through in order to deal with his injuries must include the child. As the soldier continues to deal with the injuries he has received from the war zone, so will the child have to deal with a parent who is not the same as who he was when he left home.

This is another reason why it is very important for the community to support a returning soldier. This community needs to support the family, as they are caught between living their daily lives and relating to a loved one who may have changed both mentally and physically.

Support from one human being to another human being is always essential to the growth of one's soul. In the situation of war, this concept can be a learning experience for those involved. Many people are given the opportunities to show support; some will and some won't.

The idea of fellow soldiers working with the children and other family members of returning soldiers is a concept that must be looked at in a new way. The ability of fellow soldiers to interact with another soldier's family is an excellent way to facilitate the acceptance of the information and experiences that have been explained to the family. This is where we see the bond between military families. It is important to utilize this bond as a healing tool. When working with the complex problems that exist in a returning soldier's life, there are many advantages to introducing the resources available between military families.

Older veterans and older military families should also be utilized, as they bring experience and examples of how life will evolve later on in the soldier's family life. They have witnessed and experienced the acclimation of fellow veterans back into the civilian world and can share practical tips with newly returning veterans.

Military families should work with the community in order to bring relief in healing not only to the returning soldier but to his family as well.

Chapter 29

IT'S HARD TO ACCLIMATE BACK INTO SOCIETY

When a soldier returns home from a conflict zone, he relishes the thought of joining his family and loved ones in a reunion of life. This is always on the soldier's mind—returning home to the safety and support of people he knows and trusts.

However, throughout time, many soldiers have returned home to learn that their actions were controversial to the public at large. In some societies, people may have complained that the majority of food was used to support the military during one of its conquests, while in other societies, people might not have understood the reason for sending their loved ones into harm's way.

The concept for the returning soldier is very simple in trying to reconnect with the life he was living before being stationed in an area where violence and death may have occurred on a daily basis.

His idea of moving forward in his life with the support of his family and community is one of the great hopes he thinks about while serving during the time of war.

What starts out as a hopeful and joyous reunion can at times turn into a nightmare of confusion, emotional upheaval, and misunderstanding when the soldier returns home.

The soldier's simple hopes and dreams are at times dashed when the realization occurs to him that the community or nation was not behind his involvement in the conflict. While many times warriors returned home to heroes' welcomes and were treated with the utmost respect and honor, other times the returning soldiers were put into a state of confusion trying to deal with a conflicted civilian population.

While the soldier may be acutely aware of the experiences he has just lived through, many civilians have no idea, and this in itself causes problems. When a soldier returns home and feels as though he is disrespected, he can become agitated, unsure of himself, and open to frustration. The problems that the soldier might have to deal with while acclimating back to civilian life can be increased by the additional uncertainty of the civilians around him when at home.

While the mind and spirit try to deal with the conflict related to what the soldier has experienced, it can add to the complications of having to deal with the supposedly safe and nurturing environment that is not there.

The returning soldier may also be thinking of friends and colleagues whom he has left behind in a war zone and begin to realize that they are the only ones who can understand what he has been through. The soldier, while dealing with civilians who have not accepted or do not care about a war effort, will try to explain how his friends are still being killed and maimed. He will try to shine a spotlight on the fact that these soldiers are in need of support, and he has a hard time understanding the lack of compassion and comfort that the community is showing. It can be very frustrating for the returning soldier to have to deal with the lackadaisical attitudes of the masses while the only thing he wants is to be accepted back to his home.

He tries to reason with them by saying he didn't start the conflict—he helped when the community and nation needed him—and he just wants the respect that is due him for putting his life on hold in order to serve his country. Having to fight an enemy in foreboding locations and dealing with all the stress involved in a violent conflict and then having to come home and try to deal with this senseless reaction of civilians can cause great emotional stress, physical problems, and a breakdown of the spirit.

Many soldiers may agree or disagree about the values of the conflict they are involved in. They may begin their involvement with one set of expectations and realize that things are not as they may have seemed. When returning home, their expectations will have changed in their view of the conflict, and they now may not support it. However, they still must go through the transition of coming from a war zone to a safe civilian community. And they will still have to go through the transition of expectations they were seeking when they arrived home. Even though their opinion of the conflict might have changed and may now be in accordance with the population, their acclimation back into society will still be traumatic due to the actions of the populace.

Many times we will say, "What the hell was I doing over there if you didn't want to support me? Why did I have to go?"

You come home expecting a joyous reunion, and people spit at you. I never deserved that.

We were just trying to do the right thing for our country, and people treated us like shit.

If I had to do it all over again, I just wouldn't go. It wasn't worth it.

But when you get to our side, you see it from a whole new perspective. There are reasons things happen that you have no idea about. Some of us were just pawns in the bigger scheme of things, while others were meant to be there and to die on the field. We went to war with hopes and dreams, and many of us never returned home. We left loved ones and children, friends and family—we walked out one night and never came back. People tell stories about us from what they have remembered in order to keep our names alive. People didn't know if their sons or fathers would come home safe. Many of us came home in pine boxes.

We were asked to die at that time, but once we got over here, we could see why we did. They didn't give us all the answers, but quite a few of them were revealed to us.

My advice to service members returning home from war is to get out often and keep busy.

Stick with your family—they're your support system.

When things get tough, don't bail out. Try to work it out.

It wasn't easy on the battlefield—why should it be easy at home? You're going to learn one way or the other, so you might as well accept what has happened and move forward in your life.

Listen, it can be very difficult for those of you who are returning home with injuries. Your life has changed, and there is nothing you can do about it, but you can learn to appreciate the simple things and be the best that you can be in your situation.

In the past, many of us who returned home with injuries were made as comfortable as possible with no hope of having a normal life again. We were taken care of and respected, and that was about it. Some of you modern soldiers will have different problems than we had. The technology we have now will increase your interaction with the outside world. This could be good or bad, depending on how you use it. Some of you may rely on this technology too much, and it could stagnate you in your ability to surpass your injury and become more involved in your life. Others will use it as a tool to enhance the healing and bridge the gap where it is needed to continue to move forward and accept new opportunities in your lives.

It's up to you to make the decision individually. It's all about acceptance. You can't move forward if you're still trying to process the experience you lived through.

Sometimes there are just no answers. Trying to find them is like a dog chasing his tail. All he is going to get is a few hairs and exhaustion.

Set your sights on new horizons. You'll be surprised at what you can achieve.

Look, a lot of guys over here are cheering you on. We're pulling for you guys—we want to see you make the transition back to civilian life a healthy and happy one.

I don't care if you were involved in the conflict 40 years ago. You can still have a happy experience with the days you have left on the Earth plane.

Now get to work and get moving. You're wasting time.

Chapter 30
SUICIDE: ENDING ONE'S OWN LIFE

Sometimes I feel like it's easier just to end my life
than it is to try to understand who I am and what's going on.

Joe, we know this is a difficult subject for many people, especially those who have been touched by the death of a loved one in this manner. Suicide is a complex event that focuses on one individual but that has repercussions beyond that individual's perspective.

You see, when a person decides to take his own life, it jeopardizes events not only in his life to come but also in the lives of people who interact and are associated with the victim.

Many times the person who takes his own life does not fully understand what is happening to him and the purpose of his life. He is confused as to the nature of his being and why it is necessary to live out his path.

When it comes to the military and people who have been in a conflict zone, suicide becomes an option that is thought about more immediately than in other situations. Some people consider it an option as if it were one of many choices. Others would never even think of it as an option or choice—it would be taken off the table.

The difference between the two is the particular makeup of each individual. Some people are more active in creating their own lives. Some will make plans, orchestrate certain events, and live their lives with purpose. Others may be confused as to what part they play in life in general. They may understand certain concepts and beliefs but will usually just follow along, learning as they go. These individuals are more apt to put suicide on the table as an option when faced with the severe corruption of understanding.

When a soldier is involved in combat, many ideas, emotions, and impressions are experienced. Some of these violent experiences will cause an array of problems within the individual. Some people will be able to acclimate back into civilian life, while others will never understand the balance between their two lives. It's as if the person has become split in his essence—one being the loving human that he had known in civilian life among friends and family, the other being the individual who takes others' lives in any manner that is necessary. The pain and suffering that he inflicted does not go unnoticed, for he will always be haunted by some of the things he has taken part in.

Soldiers return home to civilian life and begin the transition from a structured military way of life to a life that has more options and choices, and less oversight. Some people can't understand the fact that they have options and choices. Their belief systems are challenged to the point where they begin to doubt who they actually are.

This can be extremely painful to an individual. It can be isolating, creating both physical and emotional pain that lingers throughout his life. It can cause waves of despair to overtake him, and at other times the despair goes underground but is still there. When this type of chronic misunderstood event continues in one's life, some people believe that the act of suicide is a way to exit the pain.

These individuals are so used to constantly running in circles that they begin to think there are no other options or choices but the final exit. Once they assume that this act of suicide will balance the books of their life, the mechanism of destruction is the only thing that is left.

The soldier is analytical in his thinking and is not just reacting to situations, even though it may seem so by his training. He is conscious of what he is doing, even though through his training, it may look as though his reactions are automated. He is aware of the situations that he partook in during the interaction with other humans on a violent level.

It is when he consciously realizes that he is in a safe area that he will begin to analyze the situations that he was in. He will begin to judge himself on how he behaved toward other humans. He realizes that being part of a war effort does, in fact, mean the taking of another's life. However, the longer he is exposed to the actions of violence, the more susceptible he is to breaking down and feeling as if he has become a killer of men.

His basic spiritual makeup begins to feel as though it is secondary, and he becomes scared that the killer in him has overtaken the real him. This fear in itself can create chaos in the psyche of the returning soldier, resulting in constant judgment of who he thinks he really is. The reality of the situation will be on the physical level, as this is something that he can relate to in a solid manner. Some may have injuries that they can physically touch or see, while others will have vivid memories of smells and sights that will bring the violence and their participation in the destruction of others to the forefront.

Their spiritual self will still be there but will have to fight against these substantial experiences. When they consider suicide in order to relieve themselves of the burden that they have put on themselves, isolation and solitude become a welcome home. The soldiers believe that by ending their lives, they are able to start over with a clean slate. Unfortunately, this is not the case.

When a soldier takes his own life, he soon realizes that by having done so, he has closed the door to certain opportunities to grow his spiritual essence. He will be burdened with the choice he has made to end his life earlier than had been planned. He will resent the fact that he himself has taken himself away from the potential for love and growth.

He will also see the destruction he has created in those who interact with him as well his family and other loved ones. He will feel the suffering and despair that the ending of his life has caused in others. He will see the grief he has caused by taking his own life.

When a soldier passes to our side from the act of suicide, he is greeted by members of his family. When we say "family," we mean his fellow brothers in arms. Some will have taken their own lives prior to his arrival, while others will have served out their entire lives before passing of natural causes. What these individuals will do when he arrives is prepare him for seeing and experiencing the emotions that others will have of his passing.

For many soldiers, this can be a very difficult time. Seeing the grief and suffering they have inflicted on their loved ones can be as great or greater than the pain they have brought on themselves from the experiences in war. You see, once they cross over, they see a larger perspective of their life's purpose. They understand the learning experiences they went through, even those of a violent nature. They can begin to comprehend what purpose they served in these conflicts.

Their fellow soldiers will help them acclimate to the new existence. Past family and friends will also join them after a certain period of time. Much healing must occur before any spiritual growth is allowed to continue. There has to be an understanding of what causes and effects have taken place due to the act of suicide.

There is no judgment, just understanding. Seeing the larger picture and understanding what has happened is enough. This is when the soldier realizes that there were other options available before the suicide. These options were clouded in fear, doubt, and despair. The soldier could not make a reasonable choice or action because he himself was bogged down with the burden that he had put on his own shoulders.

Is a soldier responsible for his own suicide? In some ways he is, and in other ways he's not. He is not responsible because he did not have all the tools and information he needed to make a better choice. On the other hand, he had resources available to him that could have cleared up the environment enough so he could have seen these other choices.

Certain things are very important to realize when it comes to the suicide of the soldier.

Don't take this course of action—it's not necessary.

Be open to new ideas about healing yourself.

Seek out answers instead of judging yourself over and over.

Don't think you know all the answers. You think you do, but you really don't—and you don't have to.

We ask that you talk to others before considering suicide.

We ask that you listen to counselors and the deep feeling you get in your gut.

Don't let fear dictate your course of action.

You might think that your suffering will diminish with the taking of your own life, but it will only be a new chapter in your existence, and you will have to learn and understand all that is associated with that action that you have taken. You still have to learn not only the lessons you have come to the Earth plane to experience, but now you must also learn new lessons around the topic of suicide. You have added more work to your life schedule.

"Joe, after arriving on this side, by taking my own life, I can tell you it's not as easy as people think. My body no longer hurts, and I no longer have a fear of being attacked, but there are other anxieties that must be faced. The realization that I should not have taken my own life is the biggest. I realize that I have affected other people's lives by bailing out on my own.

"I know the fear and loneliness one has before taking his own life. I know that adrenaline rush that one has as he pulls the trigger and ends his life. I know what it feels like to shake at the thought of ending it all. I know what it's like to think of releasing all my burdens in a single second. All these things go through your mind when the thought of suicide enters your essence.

"But believe me, and this is no bullshit, it's not over when you hit the ground. There's a whole other world out there, and I suggest you arrive here without the added burden of trying to figure out why the hell you did it yourself. I mean, shit, I see other guys come over here, and they're off playing golf, having fun, laughing, and having a good ol' time. And then I see the poor souls who decided to skip the future and take an early exit.

"Those guys are in class all the time, and this studying is serious shit. They have to learn so much stuff over again. Yeah, Joe, I know what you're thinking—yes, it is like taking driver's ed classes on a beautiful spring day when you want to be outside with your friends. That's kind of how it is—you have an obligation and responsibility to yourself, and you can't move on with the rest of your life until this obligation is understood and worked out.

"It takes time, but you'll get past it—most do. There are a whole bunch of guys over here who have been through it. They all say don't do it. They know it's hard, they know the pain, but there are some incredible opportunities you can take to separate yourself from that despair and isolation.

"The first is to realize that what you have done is not the true you. It is part of a lesson that you will not understand until you come to our side. Don't give up in the middle of your life experience on the Earth plane. Stick it out—you could have some wonderful experiences if you allow yourself to.

"Don't let others get in your way. You have the ability and strength to conquer anything and to continue on your path of learning. You are in the midst of opportunities and choices that you have no idea you have. Step back from your grief and suffering, take a deep breath, and decide to take a turn with your life and walk down a different path. Suicide is a dead end. You don't need to choose that—there are too many other roads to be walked. Take a chance, walk the road, and opportunities will come to you.

"Peace, my brother—peace is what we can give to you from our side, but it's up to you to accept it before you arrive here.

(I asked for a name and rank.)

"Joe, I'm just a spokesman for a group of guys. We are all here together to help our brothers understand what we all went through and to help them make the right choice before they blow the opportunity that we all did."

Chapter 31

SUICIDE: UNDERSTANDING THE DEATH OF A LOVED ONE

When someone commits the act of suicide, it not only affects that person but all who interact with him. Suicide may seem like a solitary, individualistic decision, but it actually involves many people. By this, we mean that by taking one's own life, there will be repercussions felt throughout the person's network of connections. The drama of dealing with the suicide of a loved one can be overbearing and misunderstood.

In order for loved ones to understand the concept of someone close to them taking his own life, they must understand where that person is coming from. They must understand the makeup of that person at the time of the suicide. Some family members and friends will begin to blame themselves for not having been able to intercede before the act was accomplished. This is where the problems begin for the family.

It is very important for family and friends to realize that their actions or inactions have not propelled the individual to take his own life. This individual is in the mists of trying to discover who he actually is. He questions his own self and what he has to offer society. Many times the individual might be in intense pain or suffer from major depression. Physical symptoms can be exacerbated by many silent psychological events that are going on at the same time.

Trying to make sense of why a loved one has taken his own life is very difficult without having the right tools and perspective to understand the event. Many people will not be able to rationalize this decision until they see how the individual felt at that particular time before his death. This perspective may only be understood once it's your time to cross over and you have more knowledge of the surrounding events leading up to the suicide itself.

People have a tendency to begin to look at their own mortality and to bring judgment on themselves as a way to reason and find understanding for their loved one's departure. The family will begin self-analysis and cross-examination because they do not understand the process involved in the person taking his life.

There is much valuable information available to people to begin to understand what some suicidal people are going through. By accessing some of this information, family and friends can get a basic understanding of some of the physical and psychological events that may lead up to someone taking his own life.

When it comes to a soldier or someone who has been involved in conflict taking his own life, many of these psychological and physical ailments have been brought to the forefront and may be at an acute stage in which the victim felt that suicide was his only option.

As we have mentioned in an earlier explanation, the suicide participant does not have all the tools to understand his choices and options. The decision to commit suicide is taken without having access to all the available options due to a lack of proper perspective.

The last thing an active soldier or veteran would want to do is bring pain and suffering to the people he loves. He does not wish to harm anyone else, as he feels that he has already done enough damage to himself and other humans. But by committing suicide, he does bring harm and suffering to the people he loves. This is an example of how his understanding of the act does not make sense in the larger scheme of things.

You must understand that the person who is taking his own life is looking for a means to an end regarding what he perceives to be unrelenting pain, suffering, and despair. That is his belief—it is not necessarily the reality of the situation. You must understand that from where he's coming, his view of life is skewed.

It is very difficult to get an understanding of how a loved one can take his own life. You are using a reality and a set of tools to come to an understanding that the participant in the suicide has not realized. The two of you are using two different sets of reality to understand the same act.

We wish to bring you comfort and let you know that your loved one is in a safe, healing place. He is no longer alone in his thoughts and grief. He is surrounded by fellow soldiers and others who have experienced the same turmoil and who have also exited the Earth plane before their time. These fellow soldiers will help the victim acclimate to his new life on the other side. They will bring peace and understanding to the individual and help him learn all the aspects of taking his own life.

There will be much reorganizing of the person's life when he arrives on our side. He will be taught to understand the process he went through while on the Earth plane that led up to the decision to end his life. From our side, he will be able to see his life from a new perspective and begin to understand how events became clouded and how he was unable to make a qualified decision due to a lack of understanding or proper tools.

Once this understanding is accomplished, he will move on to other goals that he has set for his soul's growth. He will be allowed to interact with other beings in order to heal himself on many levels. He may also interact with fellow soldiers who are still living on the Earth plane in order to bring help in healing before those soldiers decide to take their own lives. This will come in various ways, such as through instinct, dreams, and other individuals who will interact on their behalf. This is why it's very important for soldiers returning home who feel that they have problems to seek out help from counselors, professionals, and other fellow soldiers to help them deal with the situations they are going through. Some veterans who have passed over from suicide may be working through some of these helpers in order to reclaim some of the understanding and healing that is needed for their progression.

So there is good that eventually can come out of one's taking the early exit from life. But it is an extra step that one need not take in order to move forward in this soul's growth. It will alter the growth of other souls as well as they try to comprehend why their loved one has taken such an action. This ripple effect will cause much more work to be accomplished than what would normally be required.

Understand that those who have taken their own life are in helping hands.

They will receive healing and comfort while assessing what has taken place.

Don't blame yourself for your loved one's decision.

It's not important for you to understand the act, but to understand the outcome.

Don't begin to carry the burden of your loved one. This will only stunt his spiritual growth on the other side.

Release his existence with love and understanding. This will be most powerful to him.

Seek out counsel for your own questions and despair, for many of us work through them in order to continue to grow on the spiritual level.

You don't have to go it alone. Talk to others and learn to become strong.

Do not miss your own opportunities in life by trying to understand something that you will not truly comprehend until you reach the other side.

"Hi, Joe, my name is Maria. My son committed suicide while I was at work. I didn't know he had the troubles and thoughts that would lead up to him taking his own life. We thought he was unhappy at times because of some of the things he had done overseas. He did drink a lot but not to excess. He seemed to get along with his friends, and we were totally surprised when it happened.

"When we looked back, we could see that there were many signs that he was having a difficult time. We asked ourselves why we could not have seen such signs and helped him before it got to that point. But we just didn't know what was going on inside his head.

"He told us he was suffering from blackouts and posttraumatic stress syndrome. We had no idea to what extent these events affected him. We knew he had seen combat and had been involved in killing others, but so had his whole unit, and others seemed fine when they came back. He even joked that it was a piece of cake. We didn't know he had difficulty dealing with what happened over there. He just told us that it was "no biggie mom." He didn't lead on that anything was really wrong. But now we know better.

"After passing away from a bout with cancer, I can see the turmoil that he experienced while he was in the war, and I can understand why he felt the way he did before he took his own life. I had no idea about the despair and challenges he faced when he came home. There was no way for us to know this, just no way you can see inside someone's head. But once I arrived over here, I had the ability to sense and feel what he experienced firsthand. What a different perspective I had—it's difficult to comprehend.

"I see my son quite often over here, but he is very busy these days. He has much to accomplish in order to get back on the road he wanted to take. He has many guys who support him and help him understand why he took his own life. He is well loved and is healing quickly.

"I get to talk to him once in a while to say hi and to tell him I now understand what he went through and that I still love him.

He's begun to work with others on the Earth plane to help them understand that the process of suicide is not the answer.

"Joe, I would like to take this time to tell other mothers who have experienced the death of their sons by suicide that they cannot understand the process fully until they make their own transition to the other side. It is not your fault you cannot understand what's going on in your son's mind from the limited perspective you have now on the Earth plane.

"Please understand this, you can begin the healing process as soon as you accept this. Some of you cry every night for years and blame yourselves for what your sons have done. This is not necessary; it is a negative reaction that will affect your own life once they pass over.

"Continue to send love and prayers to your deceased loved one. This will help with his healing process. He can hear your prayers and feel your love, and it brings great comfort to him. He is in a safe place; he is with people who love him.

"What more could you ask of him? Now begin the healing process for yourself. You deserve it; he wants you to be happy—he needs you to be happy in order to relieve the suffering that he feels he has brought upon you.

"So if you wish to help him, you must begin to heal yourself because the more you suffer, the more you will bring guilt and despair to him on the other side."

Chapter 32

LEADERSHIP

Joe, to understand the role of leadership in the military, one must understand how the command structure works. Some of us were elevated through the ranks by the number of years we have been members of the military. Others received promotions for their service in the field. Some were just appointed to the position they held.

We want to focus on battlefield leadership, but we will touch upon the influences and insight of leaders higher up in the chain of command. Many times soldiers who must lead others into battle have specific concerns that others in the unit might not understand.

When a leader is in a position of making decisions, some of which are made on the spot and concern the lives of others that he is responsible for, much pressure can accumulate in this person's psyche. Some leaders can dish out orders without any ramifications to themselves. This type of leader can separate himself from his feelings toward his fellow soldiers. He focuses on the task at hand and tries to take out as much of the human element as possible. This enables him to make decisions based on tactics and goals. Otherwise, if he began to incorporate the feelings of other soldiers he was responsible for, it might skew his decision-making process and disrupt the mission.

Many leaders try to use this method to a certain degree. However, in the field of battle, many leaders who have fought bravely with their comrades will understand the feelings that the other soldiers are going through. They have fought with them on the same level, and they know the same fears, anxieties, and stress that take place before, during, and after a battle. They try to incorporate this into their decision-making process. They have orders from leaders above them that must be carried out in order to achieve the larger goals of the military. They will follow these orders as closely as possible in order to accomplish their mission.

But there are times when individual decisions must be made on the spot that will concern the possible loss of life of a friend or colleague. It is at this time that a special stress and anxiety will be noticed within the leader that the everyday soldier cannot understand. It is one thing for a soldier to have anxiety and stress concerning a battle, thinking of his own life and his loved ones back home. But when the leader makes a decision to send a friend or colleague directly into harm's way, he begins to also think about that person's life, family, and loved ones at home. It may only be for a brief moment or not even a conscious thought at the time the decision is made. However, these decisions, as they add up over time, will build up in the psychological makeup of that leader.

Many times when that leader is promoted, he will bring with him these memories and decisions that have cost many their lives.

Some will balance that with the lives that have been saved. They will rationalize the decisions based on many factors, including their own orders from above, and will work to the best of their ability to accomplish the mission with the least number of injuries and deaths. It also helps that they are still in the military branch and are surrounded by other leaders who also have been in battle and have had to make similar decisions. So their access to others to talk freely about their experiences is more open than a foot soldier returning home to civilian life.

However, leaders who leave the military and return to civilian life will experience similar symptoms of war as the foot soldier returning home. These questions, doubt, and guilt can be magnified by the fact that some of the decisions have brought others into harm's way. While the regular foot soldier will begin to judge his own actions and experiences in the war zone, the leader will begin to judge his actions and decisions that have affected his fellow soldiers.

Many times these leaders are in contact with people they have fought with in distant lands. Some of these leaders might actually have met family members of soldiers who were killed in action. They will be asked to describe the events that led up to the family members' love one losing his life. These types of interactions can be comforting on one level and very stressful on another. They can be healing for some and cause psychological damage for others.

So it is a fine line that the leader must walk while commanding soldiers. He must look out for himself and his own concerns about returning home safely as well as looking out for the concerns of the soldiers he is commanding, for he wishes to have his soldiers return home to their families and loved ones as well. A leader feels a great responsibility to those he has command over.

Oftentimes leaders are given orders that they might not agree with but have to carry out. These types of situations are often highly stressful and will remain with a leader for many years to come, for he knows that the decision to carry out the mission will definitely lead to the loss of life of some of the members of the unit that he is commanding. The leader realizes that the loss of personnel is inevitable in a war zone. However, when the leader realizes that the orders he has received will compound the situation and create more death and carnage than is necessary, he becomes agitated and helpless.

Being in the situation of the battle, he might have made a different decision on his own but may be limited due to orders he has received from a distant command. Sometimes he will feel as if his hands are tied trying to complete a mission with a rope around his neck. He feels that if he had more freedom to decide and act, he could save more of his soldiers' lives and still complete his mission. However, many times he does not have this choice. Not having this choice brings on questions of judgment and doubt.

These decisions will be thought out and revisited over and over again in the leader's mind throughout his career. When he returns home to civilian life, some of these decisions will follow him and, to a certain degree, may haunt him. He will begin to ask himself if he should have overruled a certain command in order to have protected soldiers he was responsible for. He will realize that he did not want to overrule commands from higher up, but at the same time he thought he should have made a different decision in order to save the lives of his fellow soldiers.

Here are a few comments that we have put together for the people who have experienced the responsibility of a leadership position.

Don't judge yourself for the actions that you have taken. You were working in an insular environment.

Soldiers will realize your decisions and actions once they have come to our side.

Realize that you did the best you could in a particular situation.

The leaders above you would do the best they could.

Everyone will not be on the same page on the same day.

Your actions were honorable, no matter what decision you made.

Don't forget about the learning experiences you have gained from a leadership position.

Your ability to lead should be carried forth in the civilian world in order to help others.

You can't blame yourself for the loss of life of others, for that came with the job.

"Joe, I was commander with the 16th Battalion. I fought alongside my men day after day. There wasn't a day that went by that I did not second-guess my decisions. We all have a job to do, and sometimes I had to be the bad guy. If I told soldiers to do something and it wasn't done, there'd be hell to pay. You can't have the breakdown of the unit by having soldiers dictate what course of action you're going to take. It just doesn't work like that—you would just be overrun and wiped out. The decisions we made were well thought out, and that's why they were given.

"Now after the battle was done, while the decisions were studied to see how they affected the outcome, things came up that we saw we could've done differently. But at the time of the event, you had to roll with what you got. I don't take honor in the fact that some of my decisions led to the death and destruction of my soldiers. It's a byproduct of the decision-making process.

"I understand where the soldier is coming from. I'd been there, and I know what it feels like, but there's a bigger picture that I see in order to complete a mission. Some soldiers will die in order to protect other soldiers, and as leaders we must make these decisions.

"I didn't come home in a box like many of my colleagues. But I didn't leave life on my own terms, either. I was mowed down by some idiot driving too fast; I would've thought it would've been a bullet, not an automobile.

"To the leaders who are struggling with the decisions they have made, I offer this piece of advice: Don't let it get to you—you have a job to do, just get it done. You're not going to feel any better or worse by struggling over the decision. You've been trained well, and that training will guide you through the responsibility you have for your mission and your soldiers."

Chapter 33

IT'S NOT ALL SERIOUS

Joe, when we talk about war and conflict zones, the main theme always seems to revolve around pain, suffering, and the loss of life. Much suffering that is experienced by the soldier who returns to the civilian world is caused by the interactions he has experienced in a war zone.

However, there are times of levity that are sprinkled throughout a soldier's experience in the military. And we truly enjoy these times as we watch and interact and listen to our brothers give freely of their loving essence to others around them. Laughter is indeed the best medicine. It has the ability to disrupt certain negative thinking patterns as well as change the chemical reactions within the human body. Laughter can heal on many levels and also brings the human body back into balance with its spiritual essence.

It is a coping mechanism as well as a creative expression of an individual. It is a very useful tool that needs to be accessed more freely throughout the world. It is underutilized to the detriment of society. People should learn to share more laughter with others during difficult times, for these times are when it is most necessary.

While serving in a combat situation, the weapon of laughter can balance a soldier's insecurities and fears. It will allow him to increase his energy, hope, and focus. It allows his body time to heal on the physical, emotional, and psychic levels. It should be utilized throughout the military as a tool to increase the help to the soldier. It can clear the mind of obsessive thoughts and bring back into balance one's perspective of the situation he is encountering.

This tool should also be used more in the civilian world when the soldier returns and begins to analyze the events that he experienced while serving in the military. Laughter, when added to other tools such as counseling, talking, and prayer, can have great results in resolving many of the issues that face soldiers returning from war.

You see, having the ability to look at a situation from a different perspective—in this case, a humorous perspective—allows the soldier to begin to analyze his experiences from different angles. One of the problems when soldiers begin to self-judge is that they focus on only one perspective, and that is usually to bring judgment or blame on themselves. But when the tool of laughter and humor is injected into a situation, the soldier and civilian must look at the situation from a different perspective, which will result in laughter and all its healing qualities.

Although many situations inside a war zone are cruel and inhumane, there are times when simple things may cause a smile or a break in attention in the moment. It may be glancing down and noticing a particular product or memento while walking through a destroyed building or town. It may be witnessing a fellow soldier performing a duty that is not in line with the particular situation at hand. An example of this may be a soldier cleaning himself in a shower located outside while it's raining. Someone may comment, "What's the point? Just wear a bar of soap around your neck." Something as simple as that may bring a smile or reaction from the participating soldiers that can relieve stress and give the mind a break from the constant overstimulus of a war zone.

Some may think that laughter in the face of destruction and cruelty is not appropriate. However, we are telling you that that is the place where it should be used. It should be used in extreme situations, as it will erase unhealthy thought processes and realign the mind of the soldier to be more focused on the immediate needs of the situation.

Now, there is a huge difference between laughter and humorous comments and taking advantage through cruel methods in order to get a laugh response. People who use this method to get this type of response are not using this tool effectively nor for the purpose it was created. Not only will the results be negative, but it will create more harm in the psyche of the individual later on in life.

Laughing at a crippled or disabled being is not the proper use of this tool. Many times when this happens, it is the result of a psyche that has gone haywire and is not the true face of the soldier who was participating in that event. However, there are individuals who will instigate certain events in order to create what they think is a humorous scene. Their cruel sense of humor is troubling to others and can create disharmony among the group.

One of the characteristics of the military unit is the ability to have discipline and expectations of the soldier to perform in a professional manner. Using cruelty in the disguise of humor is not professional and is a breakdown in the discipline of that group. We have witnessed this personally many times and understand that these things do happen. But when certain individuals continue with this course of action, it is necessary for someone to step forward and put an end to this process.

We realize that every soldier will have distinct memories of humorous situations that have occurred while serving in the military, from sitting on a cactus during training to forgetting one's boots before a multi-mile run.

Laughter is there for a reason.

Do not be ashamed to smile and laugh.

When you create laughter, you create healing energy.

Your mind will thank you for changing its negative pattern through humor.

Live, laugh, and dance—there's a reason why laughter is in there.

Laughter sometimes might be the only hand that pulls you up.

Laughing alone is one thing, but laughing with others creates positive rippling vibrations.

There's always time to be serious, but a smile always helps.

"Hi Joe, my name is Arnie. I was stationed with a tank battalion. I've got to tell you a story that happened to me while out on maneuvers. We just got settled in, then did all our checks, and were moving down through a set of trees into an open field.

My gunner had just released the lock on his ammo when I heard a crash and thud. We had just reached the field, and the tank had clipped the only remaining tree in the open field. We could've gone in any direction, but no, we had to hit the only damn tree that was left. We all looked at each other with shock on our faces as we realize the stupidity of the moment.

"It was no biggie in the course of our service, but it was just one moment were we really cracked up at the thought that we were in control of all this power but couldn't avoid a single lone tree in a vast field. One of the guys asked if I was busy picking my nose when we hit the tree. Another one said more like looking at my dick. Just one of those stupid things that happens that brought relaxation to us all for a brief time.

[Author] I have other soldiers here who are reacting to this story and are now confronting Arnie about hitting the tree. I can hear one of them saying, "Are you freaking kidding me—you hit a fuckin' tree in the middle of an open field?" They're all laughing among themselves—I assume because they can all relate to doing stupid things at one time or another.

"And you want me to follow up after that story? Joe, William Conrad here. Just wanted to stop by to tell you I have done some crazy shit while serving and saw a lot of funny things happen to other service members. I've seen guys walk around with their shirts on backward thinking that it was a new type of uniform—seriously, no joking! After we stopped laughing and told them, the expression on their faces made the laughter even louder. How the freak can you put a shirt on backward and think it's some type of new freakin' design? You're in the Army, for Christ's sake. Think they change the uniforms with every season, depending on the color and texture that are in style? You can't make up some of this shit.

"And I can't count how many times guys have fallen out of trucks because they were doing something stupid, like putting on their boots while the door was open and going downhill. That shit happens all the time, and some guys get hurt. I'm laughing but I shouldn't, but some of these people just don't think.

"Thanks for letting me come through and share this insight. There are a lot of smiling vets over here right now, thinking about all the situations they were involved in that cracked other people up. The energy is very light today. I feel like we'll be telling stories for quite a while."

PART III

Chapter 34

HEALING

We can give you examples of techniques that have worked in the past. We can also utilize technology that is available today. While some soldiers and civilians will be open to one method, some might respond better to others. Therefore, we will give you a menu of various techniques and ideas to help in the healing process of those who need it.

Today more than ever, we see millions of people suffering due to the consequences of war and conflict. People nowadays are more attuned to situations around the world due to technological improvements over the last decades. Where once people only heard about conflicts through secondhand observation and limited correspondence, today one can be actively involved in a conflict area at a moment's notice. The ability to transfer information while the conflict is happening has brought new considerations and consequences to those who have to deal with it.

An example of this is a soldier talking to a loved one who is home in a safe location. This contact can be sent live from a conflict area in a moment's time. In years past, written correspondence could take weeks or months to be received by a soldier's family. With the technology available today, family members and the general public have access to war zones, which they never had to deal with in the past.

It is important to take this new method of communication into consideration when dealing with problems related to the healing process. Acclimation of the soldier returning home has changed over the years, as some long ago may have taken months or even years after leaving a war zone to return to their family and homeland. Today a soldier can be a conflict zone one day and the next day be in a neutral, safe, modern city.

So we will consider all these aspects as we talk about utilizing certain healing modalities that are available to everyone concerned. For example, we will talk about how the human body has natural healing abilities that can be tapped into in order to relieve the suffering that continues once someone leaves a war zone. There are physical abilities that can also be utilized to relieve the stress and torment that challenge so many who have been involved in war.

We believe it's important to offer these techniques to those in need. It is our understanding that the release of the information in this book will, in itself, bring healing and comfort to many. This basic information that people have wondered and thought about throughout time can be used to bring understanding to certain situations and help to explain why an individual feels the way he does. It is the beginning of an individual's education to utilize and bring healing to himself.

Others will have to utilize a variety of techniques in order to achieve the level of comfort and healing that they seek. The interaction between individuals is very important to these particular people because they react in a more positive way when they interact with more than one member of the healing community.

Examples of this may include ongoing conversations in a group setting and talking one-on-one with professionals who have been trained in the theory and utilization of healing techniques. Others will be able to slowly let the information they've acquired in this book seep into their psyches and eventually bring about a peaceful healing presence within their bodies.

Healing can take place on many levels, including the physical, emotional, and spiritual levels. Soldiers and civilians who utilize some of this information can direct it toward the specific level where it's most needed. Some soldiers may feel as though they have lost their spirit; in that case, they need to be helped on the spiritual level. Others may be in a place of emotional unrest due to activities they participated in while in a war zone; in that case, the healing can primarily address the emotional level. Some of the healing information will be used to bring forth healing on multiple levels at the same time.

This information should be shared with others who may not have been in a conflict or war zone but who have suffered similarly to those who have. Civilians who have been in contact with violent activities may suffer from the same symptoms and conditions as those who have actively participated in war. Some of the information in this book will be helpful to people dealing with those issues.

We hope that the information is presented in a clear and precise way to the extent that this type of information can be transcribed. We realize that some of the questions and answers will bring out emotional responses, but we are explaining this from our perspective, which is the larger picture that we have the advantage of seeing from our side of life.

We would have periodically throughout the book given you information on how a healing process can begin, it may be tied into the particular subject or question that we are discussing at that time.

It is important to remember that the hardship that is taking place in one's life is shared by many and that the ability to help heal others is always available to oneself. It is, in fact, magnified when one helps another who is suffering. By this, we mean that the person who is giving help to one who is suffering will also receive help by this action. So is important to support your fellow man during the time of discomfort, suffering, and misunderstanding.

People sometimes have the misunderstanding that certain events should be dealt with in a certain manner in order to relieve the suffering of a particular individual. We see it as a much more complex situation. First of all, the individual is confused about the initial manifestation of symptoms throughout his being. Then there is misunderstanding at times when dealing with one's own idea of what is happening and trying to explain it to other individuals. One size does not fit all. However, many common healing techniques are available that could be used on a large scale to help many people conquer the suffering they are currently experiencing. Some things may need to be altered slightly on an individual basis, but the larger concepts that we will be dealing with in this book can be used on a large scale across a vast number of individual experiences.

Chapter 35

CONCENTRATING ON THE WHOLE SELF, NOT JUST THE PHYSICAL BODY

Joe, many times when healing is the topic of discussion, people have a tendency to focus on the physical body. We realize that the physical body is a shell that you inhabit, and it is your responsibility to watch over it. It is a means for you to live in the environment of the Earth plane. It is made up of structures of matter from the surrounding environment and is programmed to let you know when it needs certain things in order to continue to house your spirit entity.

Some of these signals may be as simple as hunger, which tells you that the body needs nourishment. Some may include the sensation of pain, which makes you become aware of a condition that is affecting the structure of the body. This can be internal or external and is basically a warning device to prompt you to take action.

Many different levels of disease and injury to the body can cause additional pain and suffering to the emotional and psychological parts of your body. The physical body interacts with the other parts of your being. The physical structure interacts with your emotional essence, your psychological makeup, and even your true spiritual core. They all work together in the structure that you call the human body.

Consequently, when healing is to take place, it must include all of these areas of the body, as they are all interdependent. You may not realize that a physical injury is related to a psychological problem or that emotional distress can cause physical injuries. But at some level, all of these will have some impact on the suffering, pain, and injuries that an individual experiences. Healing will also affect multiple areas at the same time, even though an injury or disease is affecting only one area.

Recently on your side, you have discovered techniques and diagnostic tools that show the interaction of these different areas of your existence. People realize that the emotional and psychological health of the human can affect physical abilities. A simple example of this involves stress and anxiety, for they will cause physical symptoms to appear that disrupt the physical body. The stress and anxiety will be located in an area that is not of the physical body but is essentially interconnected with it.

So when attempting to bring healing to a particular area of the human body, it is important to focus on the entire body and all areas of that being. If you only focus on one particular area—the obvious area to some—you may not be able to achieve true healing but rather only brief relief from the symptoms that have appeared.

For example, for many years people have realized that individuals heal more efficiently in a peaceful environment. This is an easy way to see how the different areas of the body interact with each other. Some will say that because of this peaceful environment, one's blood pressure and other chemical reactions in the body are more easily stabilized. Although this is true, other unnoticed healing is also occurring in other parts of the body.

In dealing with the healing of the human body, you need to focus on three steps:

The ability of the individual to realize that he or she is made up of separate yet collective parts

The realization that healing on just one level may not be enough to heal the situation at hand

The realization that healing in one area can cause healing in a totally different area.

These three simple explanations should always be held in the back of your mind when healing needs to occur. If you are aware of how different parts and areas of the body interact with each other, it will open the pathways for the communication of healing to interact within these areas. Just being aware of the makeup of your body is of vital importance.

Your spiritual essence is the driving force in your life's learning process. It is the moral compass that each of you has within you. Some may call this a gut instinct, a mother's intuition, or perhaps just a sense of right and wrong.

Your spiritual essence will design the learning experiences that you have come to witness and participate in. It will interact with the human body in order for these lessons to be played out. Sometimes these lessons will involve the deterioration of the body in order to facilitate a particular learning experience.

Some may ask why a certain thing happens to them, and this is the reason. They are meant to experience this particular event in order for the spiritual essence to learn and also to help teach others very valuable lessons. Some of these lessons include the ability to show compassion and empathy and to put others before themselves.

However, many times the physical body will begin to break down before certain lessons have been completed. At those times, a person's life lessons can be altered in order to achieve certain lessons that have been planned out, but in a shorter period of time. These lessons can also be altered to work with a body that is not functioning at a proper level.

There are times when healing will take place in order to bring the body back into a proper position to carry on the learning that the spirit has come to expect. This healing may happen automatically, as it is preprogrammed into your physical structure for certain reactions to happen, such as your natural ability to fight certain diseases. The body comes with many valuable tools that can be used on an automatic basis to correct situations that may be harmful to the human being.

Other times, outside influences must be utilized in order to bring the body back into proper balance. These outside influences will occur in interactions with other humans or through the individual's own focus on connecting to a higher source in order for the healing to occur.

We advise you to use all the necessary tools in order to achieve the proper balance and harmony of the body. Is important for an individual to use the tools that have been given to him in order to prosper. Some of these tools include the power of laughter and the ability to pray, which is a form of communication from the individual to either his higher self or the spirit realm, where many of his guides and loved ones are able to interact with him.

By looking at the body as separate areas that are all interacting, it is easier to heal when one understands that it can occur on many different levels. When an individual is ill, he can tap into his own tools in order to analyze and possibly initiate healing himself. He may decide to utilize the services of others who have more experience in being able to bring healing to the human body. These individuals may specialize in different areas of the body where the healing needs to take place.

It is important at this level of healing that specialists learn to work together. If one specialist focuses on the physical body while another specialist focuses on the emotional state of that individual, it is important that the two of them communicate with each other to bring their work with that individual into a state of balance. At the same time, is very important that the spiritual needs of the individual are looked after. We see this many times—that this part of the healing process is left vacant. People often believe that if you cannot feel, touch, or correct something physically, it doesn't need to be involved.

The spiritual health of an individual is paramount throughout his entire life. The individual must actively participate in this spiritual health. He can do this through meditation, self-analysis, and connecting to the spiritual realm from which he came.

There are individuals who have a great deal of experience with the spiritual realm who can bring advice, understanding, and knowledge to the individual in order for his essence to stay in good health. We ask that the spiritual health of an individual be instituted from the day of birth. The sooner this is learned and accepted, the easier it will be to implement the healing techniques. Once the individual realizes that he is made up of a spiritual essence, he will be able to tap into its power much more easily.

The spiritual essence has the ability to magnify any healing process. It can decide how the healing will take place and in what time frame. It can rewrite the person's spiritual life lessons. In order to do this, it will shift the status of the human condition. If certain needs must be met in order to learn from an experience, the body will be allowed to heal at an amazing rate.

But it is vitally important for an individual to realize that he has this power within himself. By accepting this power and using it, the individual becomes more comfortable with himself and his life's experiences.

All the medical knowledge in the world cannot help an individual who suffers from a spiritual disruption. This is why it is extremely important to focus on the spiritual core of an individual, as this is the most important area of human existence.

We ask that you share this knowledge with others so it may become ingrained at all levels of society and so that people will learn and understand this interdependence at an early age.

Chapter 36

THE PHYSICAL TOUR ENDS, AND YOUR NEW SPIRITUAL TOUR BEGINS

Joe, it has been our honor to take your readers on a journey of exploration and understanding. We have tried to send this information many times before, and some bits have been received, while others never made their way to the Earth plane. With this attempt, we feel as though we have achieved our mission in its entirety.

It is important for your readers to understand that the information we have distilled on your side is to be used to bring comfort and healing to those who are most in need. It should not be manipulated or used to the advantage of one group over another.

At the beginning of the book, we explained how the soldier is not just a physical being placed in an area of conflict but rather is a spiritual entity who has chosen to participate in the physical world. Once the understanding is achieved that the soldier himself is truly a spiritual energy, he can begin to move forward from the experiences he lived through during the time of war.

For it is in the knowledge that the true you is of a spiritual nature that healing and growth can proceed forward on the path that was meant to be. Once the soldier moves beyond this physical realm and begins to see the bigger picture of his life and understands his true makeup, the opportunities for growth, learning, and teaching will multiply.

If a soldier does not wish to take into account his true identity and wishes to stay bound to the acceptance of his perceived limited physical makeup, his opportunities for growth and learning will be limited.

Your physical tour of duty ends when you accept the fact that you are a spiritual being. A new spiritual tour begins a process of internal growth and prosperity. The growth opportunities are unlimited, and so is the ability to teach others what you have learned. Very few reach this stage while still living on the Earth plane. You will have this opportunity to help others while still learning your own lessons before it is your time to return home to our side.

Others will have to wait until they have crossed over and have the ability to see with a new perspective how they have grown and interacted during their time on the Earth plane. At this time, some will be allowed to help others who will now be living their lessons in a conflict zone.

Joe, so many people have been involved in the writing of this book who have wanted to participate in the transfer of this knowledge and to be part of a project that can bring comfort and healing to their brothers in arms. These soldiers here have tremendous respect and admiration for all those who are currently serving or who suffer from the environment of war zones. So much love and compassion come from their essence that they want to share with those in need on your side.

Many examples we have used in this book have been taken from personal situations, while others have been general feelings and experiences of the majority of the soldiers who helped bring forth this information.

It's not rocket science—we know you've heard some of this before, but maybe you should start listening to it. We know what we're talking about, and we see the suffering you guys are putting up with every day. You're all going to learn it eventually, so why not start now while you're still there? Tell your friends about it, talk about it openly, and share this information.

What do you care what people think? It's your life. It's like driving a fancy sports car—you don't want to be in the passenger seat; you want to be behind the wheel, and that's your life. Take the wheel, open it up, and take yourself to places you've never been before.

Your adventure begins the moment you accept who you truly are. You are a part of God, and you are a spirit of tremendous energy, love, and compassion. Now take that beauty on the road and don't look back. Live your life like it's the only one you have, 'cause it is.

Welcome back, welcome home. Now live, live, live!

Chapter 37
AUTHOR COMMENTS

It's our responsibility—as individuals and as a nation

I want to take this opportunity to express some of my personal feelings concerning our servicemen and women. I think it is extremely important for all of us—as individuals and as a nation—to support our servicemen and women at every level. At times it seems easier to wave the flag and put a sticker on one's car than to make an authentic sacrifice in support of soldiers and veterans.

National security and war can be messy situations, to say the least. Too many times, the truth of the cost of conflict—physically, mentally, and financially—is hidden from us. We are now seeing the cost in terms of returning soldiers, as many return with physical and mental disabilities that, in past wars, might not have allowed them to make it home at all. Are we prepared to accept our fellow citizens who have sacrificed so much for us? Are we prepared to make our sacrifice—in time, money, and support?

We cannot carve out sections of our society to participate in a war and let them fight it for us while we go about our daily lives with as little participation as possible. We as individuals and as a nation need to have a little more skin in the game, as the saying goes. We need to make more personal sacrifices—the ones that hurt, the ones that make us uneasy, the ones that grab our focus. It's time to put down the TV clicker and our addiction to reality TV shows and become involved in the lives of our veterans who need our help, for they were there for us, to help us in various ways, both regarding security and in actual combat, while we sat at home in a safe, secure environment.

All veterans should have the best quality of health care and job opportunities for themselves and their families. If a veteran is disabled, he should be cared for, and his family should be helped with any resources that are needed. This should not be a political football—it should not be used by others to manipulate situations. Veterans served, they put in their time, and now it's time for our sacrifice.

When I look at the culture that surrounds us, with the vast amounts of money going to celebrities, sports teams, and other aspects of our society, I ask why there is any debate concerning the treatment of our soldiers and veterans. I think most of us can agree that some simple sacrifices on our part are not asking too much. Unfortunately, this area of support is ripe for miscalculations, misappropriations, and political fodder.

I'm a big believer in giving soldiers the right tools for the job. You don't send a soldier to a war zone without proper equipment, as we saw in the earlier parts of the Iraq and Afghanistan wars. To me, there is no excuse for that bullshit. Soldiers were lost due to the ineptness of people higher up.

When our nation was at war during World War II, we had plants and shipbuilders working 24 hours a day. The nation itself worked as a whole in order to provide for soldiers. Maybe that explains why, back in those times, veterans were treated with much more respect and were given greater access to the services they needed—because every day, millions of people wanted to work to support them. Nowadays, however, limited corporations have exclusive contracts to provide certain materials and supplies.

When I used to read about the lack of protection some of the Humvees had and how they began to add extra plates and mechanisms in order to protect the soldiers they carried, I was stunned to learn how long it would take to get some of these new vehicles into the war zone. I thought more soldiers would be killed, and they were because of the delay. There just doesn't seem to be the same accountability that was there in the past.

I fear that we, as individuals and as a nation as a whole, have basically been victims of smokescreens and have been fed nightly entertainment shows while the business of war has raged on for more than a decade.

We, as individuals and as a nation, must be vigilant in ensuring that our soldiers and veterans are not used for political and financial gain. We should not tolerate our fellow citizens being used and left to face the after-war burden we see so many now trying to live through.

Are our soldiers allowed to win today's wars in a timely manner? I don't believe so. I believe there is too much money involved in dragging out conflicts that could be ended much sooner. The military currently has the technology and the ability to take advantage in a war zone to the extent that much can be accomplished in a short period of time. However, the longer a conflict drags on, the more someone is making money. We as a nation are paying for it in broken bodies and broken minds.

We are the greatest nation that has ever populated Earth. We protect our citizens as well as people of other societies who do not have the strength to fight their aggressors. We help cultures and societies after wars, and we try to bring peace and understanding to regions that are currently experiencing disruption. We need to stay vigilant as individuals and as a nation to our goals and responsibilities.

Our responsibilities to our soldiers and veterans are equal, whether they are in the field or have returned home. I ask everyone to make a sacrifice on behalf of fellow citizen veterans in any way you can. I also ask that all of us stand up and speak out in support of our veterans. This must be done at the beginning, during, and at the end of every conflict. We must ask for accountability from our leaders.

One of the greatest sacrifices we can make is to question our leaders with regard to their decisions and actions concerning our involvement in war. Let no man or woman stand before us and tell us it is unpatriotic to state our case. It is the most patriotic thing that individuals can do to hold their leaders accountable for the decisions they make that will affect neighbors, colleagues, and loved ones.

It has been an honor to work with the deceased vets from the other side and to bring forth this valuable knowledge to our Earth plane. I will continue to do whatever I can to support my fellow citizens in bringing hope and healing to those in need.

Chapter 38

ALWAYS CONNECTED

We want to convey to everyone the knowledge that each and every one of you is always connected. You are all connected on a spiritual level. And yes, you are all connected on a physical level. On a physical level, you all share the same physical plane. At this time, you all live on a living structure you call Earth; in the future, you will share living on other structures. Your physical bodies basically consist of all the same elements, so there are many common connections between you and every other physical being with whom you interact.

On a spiritual level, which is much broader than the physical level, you share similar attributes. You share a similar spiritual existence. The makeup of your spiritual being is similar to that of others with whom you interact, and your ability to learn and create experiences is similar to that of others.

So not only are you connected on the physical and spiritual levels, but you must realize that at no time are you alone. We realize that there are times in people's lives when they feel as if they're totally alone, both physically and spiritually. This is never the case. You are always interacting with others, either physically or spiritually and either consciously or subconsciously.

Your spiritual entities are in constant contact with others on our plane who help guide you through your existence and journey on the Earth plane. There is never a time when you are alone on your journey and do not have access to help from others on our plane. You are always connected, you always have been connected, and you always will be connected.

The opportunity of learning, growth, and experience cannot be achieved without the interconnectivity of the physical and spiritual realms. Each of you is part of this interconnectivity. It may be hard for some to understand, but you as an individual are connected to a stranger who may be on the other side of the world whom you have never met or even know of his or her existence. You may not realize that you are connected to an entity who has lived in the past or who will live in the future. For you are always connected.

As you begin to realize this connection you have with others on the Earth plane and the connection you have with the spiritual realm, you'll realize the true essence that is you.

You are a complex being of a spiritual nature who has the ability to live and experience life in multiple dimensions at the same time. And all these experiences are all connected, on all levels, at all times.

HEALING STATEMENTS GUIDE

Guidance from deceased vets in response to individual Q&As

I'm afraid that what I've done has changed me

- *Accepting change is the primary goal of self-actualization.*

- *Replace the fear of who you believe you have become with an awareness that your experiences have opened your mind to greater learning experiences that could not have been achieved any other way.*

- *It is important to realize that who you are as a spiritual being has not changed. Only the experiences you have witnessed and live through have changed.*

- *Use the experiences you have witnessed and been involved with as a positive stepping-stone to new experiences. These new experiences can give you the opportunity to bring love and understanding to others around you.*

- *Having experienced certain situations within a war will give you the opportunity to learn to love yourself to a higher degree and to be able to bring relief from suffering to others.*

I can't comprehend the things I saw

- *Any setback in a recovery is NOT a failure.*
- *Take conscious action for how you feel.*
- *Remember, some days will be more difficult than others. This is okay.*
- *Ask for help at the first sign of a setback.*
- *It's a process; it takes time, sooner for some, later for others. But at least be on the journey.*
- *Don't look back; otherwise you will trip and stumble into your future.*
- *The things that you have witnessed and experienced are what they are. There doesn't have to be an explanation.*
- *For those who cannot let the trauma go, accept it, and even take it with you, but put it somewhere where you're not going to be tripping over it all the time.*
- *Don't judge yourself. You're not qualified.*

Some people think I'm a hero, sometimes I think I'm just crazy

- *By being involved in the conflict, you have shown courage.*
- *Taking on this learning lesson is the sign of a hero to us.*
- *Realizing and accepting that you have participated under extreme conditions is important.*

We all don't feel this way, but some of us do

- *Understand that it is okay to feel the way you do.*
- *No one has the authority to tell you how you should or should not feel.*
- *You should not judge others with your perspective on how they should feel.*
- *Bring comfort to those in need, even if you do not understand their difficulties.*

Am I less of a soldier if I did not see hand-to-hand combat?

- *Once a soldier, always a soldier.*
- *One cannot engage in war by themselves.*

Relationships and how they're affected

- *Try to understand that things will be different, and that's okay.*
- *Some relationships will blossom, and some will deteriorate, but there is always hope.*
- *Understanding what someone has been through is not as important as supporting that person as an individual.*
- *If each of you backs up the other, success is assured.*
- *You will change. Accept that as the first step.*
- *There are new learning opportunities when stress is placed on a relationship.*
- *Help is available—seek it.*
- *Don't judge a broken relationship. It may be meant as a learning experience.*

Will God judge me for killing others?

- *Don't be too harsh on yourself. You'll eventually find deeper meaning in your actions.*
- *Judging is the wrong word. It's more like viewing your participation in your life's Earth experiences.*
- *It's not the number of people you've killed—it's how you went about it and the intention behind the killing.*
- *There'll be worse things in life than killing an enemy combatant. Giving up on life's opportunities for learning is one of those things.*

I feel the suffering that I inflicted upon people

- *Don't act like it didn't happen—it did.*
- *Let it go and move on. Don't deny it—just release your grip on it.*
- *By continuing to hurt yourself in self-judgment, you will bring suffering and pain to the people you love.*
- *You might think it's all about you, but your friends and family feel it, too.*
- *We are not asking you to forget it—just give yourself a break.*
- *Anger is not going to solve anything. It will just increase your burden.*

Finding one's purpose after war

- *Start off with the core basis of who you want to be.*
- *Ask yourself whether what you experienced is going to hold you back or propel you forward.*
- *Take your newfound skills and use them to determine your future.*
- *Don't let fear and inaction frighten you into not making a choice.*
- *Reach out and help fellow soldiers in making their decisions.*
- *Whatever choice you make is the right choice at that time.*
- *Stay healthy physically, mentally, emotionally, and spiritually.*
- *Take your new life in small pieces; otherwise, you may become overwhelmed.*
- *It's not always easy, but that's okay.*

How helping others can help you heal

- *Don't hold back your feelings when giving to others.*
- *Don't get upset if others shun your efforts.*
- *Don't think it'll be easy every time you extend a helping hand.*
- *By helping others, you will achieve a great resource within your spirit.*

- *Let giving be part of the new you.*
- *Giving can be physical help, emotional support, and spiritual understanding.*
- *Don't give just for the sake of giving. Give from your heart and the healing will magnify itself.*

How anxiety and stress can be disruptive to the learning process

- *Do not relate new experiences with older traumatic events.*
- *Try to separate your time of service from the events in your civilian life.*
- *It is okay to have stress. There is a purpose for it, but there is no room for chronic stress.*
- *Allow yourself to enjoy new experiences to the fullest.*
- *If anxiety and fear cripple your ability to maintain happiness, seek out help—it's your right.*
- *Leave fear and anxiety where they belong—in the past, with the traumatic event.*
- *Don't bring the baggage of the past into your future, for you will have no room for the new experiences that might bring you great joy and more understanding of who you actually are.*

POW/MIA

- *Realize that the situation herein is meant to be.*
- *Don't take it personally—there are other factors at play.*
- *We watch over you every minute of the day.*
- *We hear your prayers, your suffering, and your pleas for assistance.*
- *We need you to realize that there are others who are working on your behalf.*
- *However the situation plays out, it will be a learning experience.*
- *Helping a fellow POW can be healing in itself.*

Dealing with injuries

- *Do not despair over your injury.*
- *There is a greater good that will come out of your injury.*
- *You are helping teach others due to your injury.*
- *We are watching over all the injured.*
- *Silent injuries are as real as physical ones.*
- *We work directly with unconscious and mentally injured individuals.*
- *Don't wish for death over your injury. There are more opportunities for growth.*

Why did I go to war?

- *Your decision to become involved was made in the past.*
- *You could not have predicted the experiences you were involved in.*
- *You had honorable intentions when you decided to become involved.*
- *Your perspective has now changed—so should your expectations.*

Feeling guilty, feeling nothing

- *Some soldiers are meant to die in combat. Their deaths have meaning, even though others may not understand it at the present time.*
- *Some soldiers are meant to witness the passing of a fellow soldier in order to achieve the foundation of future learning experiences.*
- *There are reasons why things happen that you will never understand on the Earth plane.*
- *Carrying guilt and emotional stress for a long period of time will disrupt future learning experiences for each individual.*
- *We don't mind you missing us, but don't screw up the rest of your life.*
- *Let go of the baggage you carry—it's not worth it. We see this from the other side.*

- *We hear your prayers and conversation but want you to enjoy your life, so move on, soldier.*

- *As we have said before and will say again: Let it go, let it go.*

As a civilian, how can I talk to a combat soldier when he comes home?

- *Complex questions cannot be answered in smalltalk.*

- *Don't ask us if we've killed anyone. That's very personal.*

- *Ask us about common themes such as living conditions, food, and environment.*

- *We will want to tell you of more personal experiences, but you might have to wait some time.*

- *Don't ask us about our feelings right away because we are still trying to figure them out.*

- *We can't help what we have experienced and are sometimes afraid that we will be judged.*

- *Ask us about our friends and fellow soldiers in the unit. This will show how we are bound to our fellow soldiers.*

- *I know I have to mow the lawn, but some days I might be preoccupied with things from the war.*

- *Don't take it personally—just give me space. Sometimes I need to be alone.*

- *The kids are fine. They'll understand as they get older.*

- *Don't be angry at the condition of my body. Just be happy that I am home safe.*

- *If you want to know the truth, I will tell you, but don't try to change it to make it sound okay.*

- *It happened, it's over, let's move on.*

It's hard to acclimate back into society

- *My advice to service members returning home from war is to get out often and keep busy.*
- *Stick with your family—they're your support system.*
- *When things get tough, don't bail out. Try to work it out.*
- *It's up to you to make the decision individually. It's all about acceptance. You can't move forward if you're still trying to process the experience you lived through.*
- *Sometimes there are just no answers. Trying to find them is like a dog chasing his tail. All he is going to get is a few hairs and exhaustion.*
- *Set your sights on new horizons. You'll be surprised at what you can achieve.*

Suicide: Ending one's own life

- *Don't take this course of action—it's not necessary.*
- *Be open to new ideas on healing yourself.*
- *Seek out answers instead of judging yourself over and over.*
- *Don't think you know all the answers. You think you do, but you really don't—and you don't have to.*
- *We ask that you talk to others before considering suicide.*
- *We ask that you listen to counselors and the deep feeling you get in your gut.*
- *Don't let fear dictate your course of action.*

Suicide: Understanding the death of a loved one

- *Understand that those who have taken their own life are in helping hands.*
- *They will receive healing and comfort while assessing what has taken place.*
- *Don't blame yourself for your loved one's decision.*

- *It's not important for you to understand the act, but to understand the outcome.*
- *Don't begin to carry the burden of your loved one. This will only stunt his spiritual growth on the other side.*
- *Release his existence with love and understanding. This will be most powerful to him.*
- *Seek out counsel for your own questions and despair, for many of us work through them in order to continue to grow on the spiritual level.*
- *You don't have to go it alone. Talk to others and learn to become strong.*
- *Do not miss your own opportunities in life by trying to understand something that you will not truly comprehend until you reach the other side.*

Leadership

- *Don't judge yourself for the actions that you have taken. You were working in an insular environment.*
- *Soldiers will realize your decisions and actions once they have come to our side.*
- *Realize that you did the best you could in a particular situation.*
- *The leaders above you would do the best they could.*
- *Everyone will not be on the same page on the same day.*
- *Your actions were honorable, no matter what decision you made.*
- *Don't forget about the learning experiences you have gained from a leadership position.*
- *Your ability to lead should be carried forth in the civilian world in order to help others.*
- *You can't blame yourself for the loss of life of others, for that came with the job.*

It's not all serious

- *Laughter is there for a reason.*
- *Do not be ashamed to smile and laugh.*
- *When you create laughter, you create healing energy.*
- *Your mind will thank you for changing its negative pattern through humor.*
- *Live, laugh, and dance—there's a reason why laughter is in there.*
- *Laughter sometimes might be the only hand that pulls you up.*
- *Laughing alone is one thing, but laughing with others creates positive rippling vibrations.*
- *There's always time to be serious, but a smile always helps.*

PART IV

WEBSITES

Web Site
www.Joehiggins.com

Web Blog
Guidance from a Higher Plane
www.josephmhiggins.com/blog/

Make sure to sign up on the Web site to receive
• Your free "Carry Along Guidance Reference Card"
• Discounts on future products and services

Hello ... Anyone Home?
A Guide on How Our Deceased Loved Ones Try to Contact Us Through the Use of Signs

by

Joseph M. Higgins

Channeled insight and support from the author's guides and teachers will illuminate for you the steps by which the "other side" can communicate with every individual and how you can communicate with them!

* Have you ever dreamed of departed loved ones?
* Is it possible for the dead to communicate with us?
* Have you ever experienced smells, sounds, or electrical phenomena around you after the passing of a friend, family member, or colleague?

These might be signs that they are trying to contact you to let you know that they continue to be available to you. This book, *Hello...Anyone Home?* will teach you how to understand the process by which signs are given and received after the change known as death.

"Lastly I really liked how this book will make people feel more open to talking to others about the experiences that they have had or are having or will be having."
—Now Awakened | 7 reviewers made a similar statement

"This book lets us know that we are likely not crazy, and that these "signs" truly are our deceased loved ones speaking to us in one way or another."
—L663 | 8 reviewers made a similar statement

"Part One of the book starts out with the statement "They Are Always with You" in bold letters."
—Robin Landry

Available at www.amazon.com and wherever books are sold.

Available on E-readers and Audio

The Everything Guide to Evidence of the Afterlife:
A Scientific Approach to Proving the Existence of Life after Death (Everything Series)

by

Joseph M. Higgins & Chuck Bergman

Is there life after death? Or is the end of our physical existence really the end of us? In this thought-provoking guide, you will examine scientific evidence so you can decide for yourself whether or not there is an afterlife. Medium Joseph M. Higgins and "Psychic Cop" Chuck Bergman attempt to answer questions like:

* Does consciousness survive death?

* Is communication possible between the living and the dead?

* Are mediums real—or frauds?

* What happens to us during near-death experiences?

* Where do we go when we die?

* Are heaven and hell actualities?

* What is life like after death?

* Is reincarnation real—and is everyone reincarnated?

Including an overview of various religious afterlife traditions, *The Everything Guide to Evidence of the Afterlife* introduces you to the unlimited possibilities of what we face after our release from the physical world.

Available at www.amazon.com and wherever books are sold.

Available on E-readers

Made in the USA
Charleston, SC
21 May 2013